BLACKMA
THE DEATH OF RUSSIA

In all that we do in life we brave the pain
Continue to hate
Tell lies

We do not see the destruction of self
The destruction of land
Life
Hence we live to die
Fail
Never to be seen again.

Michelle Jean

To my readers, in all that I was trying to do, I was trying to avoid from writing this book. I so do not want to write it but I have to. At times it's not what you want but what you are compelled to do. Yes this book will be harsh and I so do not want it or need it to be, but must be.

Also note, this book is also an overview because it does not go in-depth about Russia. It cannot for some strange reason. Oh well, Good God has his reasons.

Trust me it is better to know the truth on earth rather than hear it (the truth) in the grave because it will be too late for you.

The truth is water hence the beginning of life starts with water. When we the children or messengers of Good God see water coming in on evil, (wicked and evil people that has and have died), we see water. Hence the dead – wicked and evil people (dead) cry out to the living and say, "***<u>WATER IS COMING IN ON THEM.</u>***" ***The water that is coming in on them is the truth that they are receiving hence they cry out to the living for rescue – saving. Now you know the full truth about spiritual water. So let no one fool you or tell you otherwise.***

2

If you are wicked and evil you will be hit with the truth in the grave and there is no rescuing for you. You will see your life in hell as well as see your eventual death. That death is reflected by the downward triangle and eye.

This book is a bit odd but its reality because I am going to touch on Russia for which I truly don't want to, but have to. Hopefully this book will be no more than 32 pages but from the way I am writing it will be more.

Russia where do I begin? Let's start with the dream I had.

In all I do, I do in truth not just for me but for you also Good God.

In all I receive, I share it with you in goodness and truth. I cannot alter the path or course of the dreams given to me. I must tell them as I see them – get them. I cannot butter anything up, nor can I give false hope. And as our days are numbered on earth, we must remain good and true to each other if we want to be saved – survive.

The shadows come now
Man's destined downfall
The sins of time
Our own doing

3

As the meteors come
Plagues join
Diseases come
Resurface
Food gone from earth – man
Cannibalism shines – take fold
We did not see the writings on the wall
We did not heed the warning signs
We thought the messengers foolish. We did not want to stop sinning. So we slaughtered the messengers of Good God for our own sins – greed.

We truly forgot the pay of sin – the wages of sin being death.

We danced like fools
Partied hard
Dined hard
Sexed hard
Hard drugs

We became the clowns in sin's court
We lay naked while sin toyed with us
Wined and dined us

We became sinful
Hence we are the naked pictures on his wall (the wall of sin) while death hold our names in his deadly book – the book of death.
Sin

4

All this we did in the eyes and sight of Good God
Now death comes
The harvest will take fold
Man – humanity will become scattered
Man – humanity will cry out to God – Good God
for mercy but no mercy will be given to him her.

We will cry out God – Good God why hath thou
forsaken me in my time of need and man –
humanity will hear too late. Humanity will be
reminded that God – Good God did not forsake
us, we are the ones to forsake life, Good God
with our willful sins hence evil WILL.

The bell tolls
The beast walks
Destruction is behind him
He takes what's his

Global Economic collapse
The collapse of Flesh
The collapse of Religion
The Devil's Empire
Sin

Waters gone
Oil dried up
Russia being the first to lose their oil – resources
Everything with them (Russia) must be tall – big
Yes powerful

But even with them, they will feel the pinch – a deadlier kind of pain and suffering – sin.

But yet they still have hope. She held one solid ripe mango in her hand. Hence there is a saving grace for Russia in all of this.

Yes it's a dream but no matter the drilling and the craters in the ground, the hose that they throw down will not find oil. Earth would have withdrawn her resources from Russia and humanity will have hell to pay after it is all said and done.

In all I dream, I see a Barren Land – the death of Russian land – civilization. And although I did not see the death of Russian people, I did see the death of the land. As if nothing grows – only wastelands. Yes I saw one with a ripe mango that was solid – firm hard. Hence I say there is a saving grace for Russia. One ripe mango had she in her hand. Yes one ripe mango had she in her hand. Hence there is a saving grace for them – Russians. One ripe mango had she in her hand hence there is a saving grace for Russia – Russians.

So to you yet again, Prokhorov truly be careful in what you do when it comes to Russia because Good God is not dicking around and he is truly watching you. You were involved in this dream yet again. So if you are not good and true to Russia in all that you do then Russia will fall and all Russians will blame you and they will have a right to. You cannot hide the truth from your people because in the dream you did not want me to tell Vladimir Putin what I saw. Hence this book I so do not want to write.

Russia is your country yes. But look at your land and the people of your land. All that evil men promise you, you will fail like them because hell is real and hell is going to be unleashed on humanity real soon. Trust me infinitely and truly on this. **HELL AWAITS THEM ALL.** Their sins have and has reached far hence the smoke I saw reaching the heavens in a previous dream. ***THIS IS THE HARVEST AND IF HUMANITY DO NOT PREPARE FOR IT THEN WOE BE UNTO THEM AND MANY WILL PERISH.*** So to you Prokhorov, truly be careful how you walk and trod with sin – evil. God – Good God is truly watching you and you are slated to lose it all – fall. You are not the only one slated to lose it all but you are the only Russian I see losing it all. Many of your counterparts in the United States are going to lose it all. Oprah is slated to lose it all because it's twice now that I've dreamt her reduced to rubble – nothing. Listen, if you do not have a good and pure heart including a clean hand Good God will not be with you. You are being warned of your danger – impending

7

downfall so truly take heed. I am not against you. This is what I saw and I am relating it back to you.

I hate to get into politics because the politics of your land is not mine nor can it be mine because I am not Russian. Life is not a game. Life is truth because Good God gave humanity good life. It is humanity to spit in God's face and take up the role and nastiness of the Babylonians. Every civilization on the planet is influenced by sin – the Babylonian way of doing things. It is in our culture, our infrastructure; our arts and crafts including designs. Your land – Russian land is no different. All I have to do is point out your infrastructure like the one above. This is evident of Babylonian rule – influence. Hence the wages of sin is death.

Like I said, I do not want to write this book but I cannot get away from writing it. I cannot go against Good God. It's unfortunate that your country will become desolate like the United States. The same fate that is going to befall them will befall your land but Russia has hope.

Like I said, ***Gog and Magog does not exist and I will not draw a correlation to the destruction of Russia based on this.*** I saw one young lady – female with a solid ripe mango hence I say Russia has hope. I know Russia does

8

not grow mangos but she had one. Hence Russia has a saving grace. You can save yourself and your land including people by walking away from the devil before it is too late. You cannot say you have not been warned because I've just warned you yet again. Walk and live not live and die. If Good God did not care about you and your land I would not be writing this book.

Yes the harvest comes
The harvest comes
Yes the harvest comes
Death walks now
Time winding down
The destruction of man – humanity

Every government will be brought to their knees

Every corrupt person will pay. Pay for his sins her sins.

Every evil society must go down to hell
Every secret society including the Elite Satanic Club must crumble. Fall down and never to rise again. All the feasting on blood and human bodies, the selling of their souls, they will find out the hard way that all the devil – Satan promised them was for naught. They will burn in hell and burn severely because their upright triangle must go down – be turned down with them.

Eve did not make it
She died and so will they

Earthly possessions are just that, earthly possessions. They will pay in hell for their disobedience. Yes they will be Satan's slaves – Abdullah's because they did sign on the dotted line. Death comes; yes death comes to collect his pay. ***HUMANITY DID SIN – WILLINGLY GAVE UP THEIR LIVES*** to die a harsh and painful death in hell alongside their father who is death.

No mansions will the super rich have because in all they did, they forgot about earth – true life that is on earth. So Russia truly think about what you are doing because at the end of it all you will pay and pay dearly if you do not walk away from sin. You must talk right, walk right; do right because you are being warned. Allelujah, you are being warned so please take heed.

It's amazing that humanity cannot figure out that the devil means them no good. I cannot understand nor comprehend why we sin when we know that when we sin we die. THE WAGES OF SIN IS DEATH BUT ***TRUTH IS***

10

EVERLASTING LIFE so live for truth and truly live.

No nation is going to win over any this I know.

No government is going to be left standing when all is said and done in this harvest. Any government that think the God of goodness and truth – Life is with them had truly better think again. The Good God of life is with none because **_GOVERNMENTS DESIGN TO LIE AND KILL - DESTROY._**

GOVERNMENTS MESS WITH THE HUMAN GNOME – DNA – GENE POOL.

GOVERNMENTS MESS UP THE FAMILY STRUCTURE.

GOVERNMENTS MESS UP THE LAND AND LANDS WE LIVE IN.

GOVERNMENTS MESS UP SOCIETY.

GOVERNMENTS MESS UP THE FAMILY CIRCLE.

IN ALL GOVERNMENTS DO, THEY MESS UP EVERYTHING.

11

There cannot be a super race – super humans or super anything because in all we do we truly kill humanity – the truth that Good God has and have given us.

In all that we do we protect the wicked and sinful – give them a home. So because of this we can only have wicked and sinful people and ***HUMANITY HAS AND HAVE PROVEN THIS IN THE EYES AND SIGHT OF GOD – GOOD GOD.*** If humans truly want and need to know about **<u>LIFE</u>** then they (you) would truly live for life and know about the atoms. There are atoms that humans cannot see with a microscope hence the technology of Good God and his children are not the same as mans. Our technology is far more advanced hence the time of God – Good God is not the time of man. Put it together if you can.

As governments you cannot send your people to war. You cannot let your people go on the battle field and kill another human being. Meaning take the flesh because the spirit of man no one can kill – take. You are wrong when you do this hence, "***<u>THOU SHALT NOT KILL.</u>***" Instead of living by this law humans – humanity kill each other daily. Then we turn around and justify our wrong doings – murderous ways with the Book of Sin – your so - called holy bible. Your book of sin specifically said, *"THOU SHALT NOT KILL"* and you go against this law. We go against the

12

law and laws of God – Good God and expect him to save us. We are going against God – Good God. So how can he save us if we have no respect for him and the law and laws he has given us to govern ourselves by?

You cannot spend billions of dollars on war games – or war machines and leave your people – citizens including children homeless and hungry. You cannot do this, it is wrong and this is why many lands are going to be left barren – wanting of food and water. This injustice, the citizens of the land can blame on you the government. You the government handed your citizens over to death on a silver platter. ***You the government made the citizens of your land including land your sacrifice unto death.***

You make the money and instead of investing the money in your people and building your land in a good and positive way, you take your money and build weapons to kill and destroy. You put your land (s) and people in debt for sin. Hence you die for sin and with sin. Let me put it this way. As you starve your people and make them suffer, your land will starve – suffer. Your land will become barren because you neglected your own. You made them starve and suffer and for this every government on earth must face the consequences because you've been found guilty of sin – hence you are guilty as charged.

13

God did not tell anyone to go out there and sin – kill.

ONE OF THE LAWS OF GOD – GOOD GOD IS, ***"THOU SHALT NOT KILL"***, but yet each and every day we kill. Hence I will forever say sin's greatest weapon against God – Good God is humanity – humans.

We have no respect for the law and laws of God but yet we expect God to have respect for us and help us.

Tell me something. Is it necessary for any country or government to spend over 43 billion dollars on war each and every year while their people go hungry and without shelter? ***TELL ME NOW, HOW ARE ANY OF YOU (POLITICIANS) GOING TO ANSWER FOR THIS GRAVE SIN?***

HENCE EVERY NATION GO AGAINST GOOD GOD AND ALL THE GOODNESS HE HAS GIVEN US.

Look at your country's national debt and tell me how are you going to pay for this willful sin? ***Your country's national debt is a sin. It is punishable by death.*** Hence in all that you do to hurt humans and land with your willful and

14

sinful wars, you the people and land must become barren – void of life – food and water.

No one on the face of this planet can justify any form of war. ***ABSOLUTELY NONE – NO ONE.*** And don't even come to me with the book of sin – your so called holy bible because that book was written by sin. Sinful and demonic people to ***SEND YOU TO HELL AND KEEP YOU IN HELL. Hence your flesh is a sacrifice unto worms and your spirit a sacrifice unto death.***

HUMANITY IS RELIGIONS SACRIFICE UNTO DEATH KNOW THAT.

YOU THE HUMAN BEING ARE THE SACRIFICIAL LAMBS UNTO DEATH AND NONE OF YOU KNOW IT UNTIL NOW.

There is no righteousness in religion hence everyone who fall under the branch or facet of religion must go to hell and burn then eventually die.

God – Good God would infinitely never ever commission a book to rob you of your soul – spirit. Especially rob you the individual of him. Please, Good God would never do this so

15

when anyone says the bible is holy I will tell you to stop lying on Good God because Good God and God did not tell anyone to lie and kill you. Lies are sins punishable by death and this is why the Babylonians are locked out of Good God's abode – kingdom. They are liars hence they deceive humanity. This is why they are called the snake. They slither like snakes hence they are the reptilians – serpent people of old.

We as humans take up crap and do it and say it is holy. The crap we take up is not holy unto life. It is holy onto death. Come on now. Yes many religions and evil people have an underlying agenda and this is wrong. We do not know what we are fighting for but yet we take up arms against the next man.

What are we truly fighting for?

The wars we make – design to kill each other will get none us to God's abode – for which some of you call paradise and heaven.

We all say we are going to see God. Now the question I ask every human being on the planet is; where is God's abode? Where is Good God.

16

Where does God live? And don't tell me God is everywhere because I infinitely truly know that God is not everywhere.

Can God – Good God be found in a dirty church or home?

Can God – Good God be found in hell where all manner of unclean people reside – is burning right now?

Can God – Good God be found amongst the wicked and evil of society – this world?

No right?

So how can you as a person say God is everywhere when we know for a fact that God is clean and not unclean? We know for an infinite fact that God cannot go into unclean places so how can we lie on God by saying God is everywhere?

If God – Good God was everywhere would the earth not be different?

If God – Good God was everywhere would there be so much killing and sins on the planet earth?

If God – Good God was everywhere, would the earth and the people of the earth not be clean?

17

We would be all clean right? So how can Good God be everywhere?

GOD – GOOD GOD IS NOT WITH MAN HENCE WE SIN AND DIE EACH AND EVERY DAY.

We have to change our dirty sheets – self by cleaning ourselves up before God – Good God can be with us and truly help us.

The earth and people of this earth are too dirty and this is why God – Good God is not with man here on earth.

As humans we have no respect of God so why should God – Good God stay amongst us or even respect us?

Good God gave us all that is good and instead of taking care of it we destroy it daily. We as humans are the ones to spit in God's face then turn around and say, "God mi sarry, please help us – me."

Why should God – Good God help any of us when we willing praise and serve death? Hence we go to war and kill others then justify it by saying they were a threat to national security. What national security?

Did you not create an insecure and unsecure nation by warring – fighting against the next man or country?

Did you not create an insecure and unsecure nation when you went against the law and laws of Good God?

Why do you think we can no longer go back to Good God or get into his kingdom – good abode?

We are the ones to give our lives over to death. So because of this, death must now take us to hell and feed us.

Sinful and wicked human beings can no longer stay on earth nor can earth – Mother Earth continue to yield her goodness unto sin's people. If she continues to do so then death must take her. Truly destroy her because she is going against Good God. She is providing death's children with a home. Maybe this is why I am seeing so many barren lands. Sin's time is up. The 24000 years that they needed is up hence earth cannot feed them or continue to provide sin's children with a home. She is breaking the law and laws of God and she too will pay if she

19

continues to do so. She must withdraw her goodness and if she does not, she will (earth will) be charged with disobedience and treason – crimes against God. This is the law and she earth cannot hide from it. Once death's children are gone from earth, the physical and spiritual realm must joint as one again meaning be on the same accord. Know that it is due to our sins that the physical and spiritual are not one, meaning on the same accord.

As humans we give up our rights to life and it is sad. Trust me I know the truth and I cannot comprehend why we would give up life for death.

Someone come along and say you must die to see God – Good God and every one of us follow blindly. Hence we failed to ask which God? Which God do we die to see?

The person that tells us that we have to die to see God conveniently omitted the most important part. ***HE/SHE OMITTED, THE ONLY GOD YOU DIE TO SEE IS DEATH.***

No one can die to see life because good life was given by God – Good God. We as human's

turned that good life into sinful life hence the
WAGES OF SIN IS DEATH.

I was taught early in my life about the casting
nets on the sea and nothing was in the net. It's
somewhere in the book of sin, your so called
holy bible. Someone please find the quote
because I don't think I quoted it exactly. Please
quote the quote exactly for me. Yes I need you to
do this. Send the quote exactly as is to Russia so
that they know exactly what I am talking about.
And fam truly thank you for your help. The
reason why this quote came to mind and has
been nagging me is because of the hose that was
thrown out or down to catch oil and no oil was
yielded to Russia. The hose is long and small in
size. The best way to describe the hose is by
using that hose commercial on television, the
blue one that curls. Better yet, the pocket hose
commercial with that small hose. The size of the
hose that they were throwing out or down the
hole was that size. This is why I say the first
place to lose their oil is Russia. This is the land
that will cast their nets and yield nothing.

People do not ask me why. This is what I saw
and this is what I am relating back to you. Many
things I've seen have and has come to pass. My
homeland I'm still waiting on to be destroyed
and it's taking so long and I so don't know why?
Yes I am getting annoyed because the

21

destruction of Jamaica will be well deserved. My homeland has and have become the modern day Sodom and Gomorrah hence the fire comes to destroy them and they don't even know it. Trust me I will feel sorry for none because Good God gave them his name including the Breath of Life and they literally spat in God's face. Hence they sin against God each and every day. You have Rasta's worshipping a mere man; an Israelite that has nothing to do with Good God. They the Rasta's claim he's a Judahite and he was never a Judahite. Jamaicans are the true Judahites because they have the name of Good God and the Breath of Life – Good Life and they tossed Good God aside to worship a man. So what happens to Jamaica now will be the people's own doing. No one on the face of the planet must feel sorry for them because they did not want or need the goodness of Good God. They had the truth and turned from the truth hence God – Good God must truly turn from them and give them what they want – that which is death. They did not want or need him Good God. Death is what they pree and want so death must take them in a brutal and deadly way.

Now as for you George Clooney you are being warned yet again. Stay the hell out of North and South Sudan because they are a BABLYLONIAN COUNTRY – NATION. _They have no respect of God because they signed their rights_ *over to death – the Arab Nation so death must take them.* **They were colonized by the Babylonians hence they speak their mother's tongue which is Urdu. So leave them alone.**

Neither you or your friend will get the oil of Sudan because the oil of the earth must dry up. It is going to dry up and there are no ands ifs or buts about this. Earth must not yield her goodness to humanity anymore. She must take away her goodness because of the sins of man. **Renewable Energy is humanity's saving grace right now** and if we refuse to get on board truly woe be unto man. **You cannot fight for a nation of people that God – Good God gave true life to and instead of keeping good life, they signed a pact with Death – the Arab League to become the slaves of death.** Trust me these lands are going to feel it so hard in the harvest they are going to more than cry. They've become ABDULLAH the servants of death. Hence Islam is not only a physical prison but a spiritual prison as well. **People will tell you Abdullah means servant of God. ABDULLAH DOES NOT MEAN SERVANT OF GOOD GOD IT MEANS SERVANT OF DEATH.** So for all the blacks that foolishly accept the name Abdullah there is repentance for you. **To name your child Abdullah is an abominable sin. It is a sin against GOOD GOD – THE GOD OF GOOD LIFE AND TRUTH. I did not know** *this until recently, hence I asked God – Good God for forgiveness and not to charge me or my son with sin because I truly did not know. Repent of this by asking God – Good God forgiveness. He will forgive you. He did me.*

You know how I know he forgave me? You're reading this book as well the other books that are written under the Michelle Jean banner.

God – Good God never made us slave. We as humans made ourselves slaves.

God – Good God never told us to be slaves to the Babylonians. We made ourselves slaves to them. Know your true history because the Babylonians were the first to enslave and colonize our asses. They raped and beat us brutally, stole our good and true history, burn our scrolls – books and gave us their perversion – sinful texts and lifestyles to kill us. ***THEY ARE AND STILL ARE THE PORK WE SHOULD NOT EAT AND ASSOCIATE WITH. THEY ARE THAT FILTHY AND NASTY IN THE PHYSICAL AND SPIRITUAL REALM.*** *This is why they tell us to eat death – pork, hence they put pork* *next to clean meats and even put it in our medicines to defile us as well as keep Good God from us.*

They raped and beat us brutally. So truly think about what you are doing George Clooney.

Black people were not the only slaves of the Babylonians. White People were slaves also. White people were brutally raped and beaten by the Babylonians so truly think of who you are defending. Africa was where life started yes. But the start of human life did not begin in Africa. Like I've said before, life began long before the conception of Adam and Eve, hence humanity – man knows not Life – Good Life. If they did, we would not be killing each other to become the CHILDREN OF THE DEAD – DEATH. Hence I will tell every European Nation that Blacks are going to charge for Slavery to tell ***THESE BLACK NATIONS TO KISS YOUR ASS AND GO FIND THEIR TRUE HISTORY AND KNOW IT.*** Blacks were not the only creation of Good God and to say Africa is the original land of Blacks and Blacks alone is infinitely wrong – false. It is a sin because Good God does not favour one race over the next. Come on now. ***THE LIFE THAT STARTED IN AFRICA – ETHIOPIA HATH NOTHING TO DO WITH MAN. WHERE LIFE MERGED IN SOUTH SUDAN***

25

HATH NOTHING TO DO WITH MAN EITHER. THIS LIFE HAS TO DO WITH WATER – THE GOODNESS OF GOOD GOD IN THE PHYSICAL AND SPIRITUAL HENCE NO HUMAN BEING ON THE FACE OF THE PLANET CAN LAY CLAIM TO GOOD GOD. NONE!!!!!!!!!!! So when any race say Good God is their right, I ask what right do any of you have to God – Good God? Humanity – Man destroy life – good life, so how can life – good life have anything to do with people that destroy it – life? This is why I tell Black people to truly know their history and STOP LYING ON GOOD GOD BECAUSE IT DOES NOT BECOME US. And don't even think of coming to me with Genesis because God – Good God did not make you in his likeness – flesh. *When you are born you look like your mother and father.* The good spirit or energy that is within you is the likeness of Good God not the flesh. Hence the spirit or soul whichever you prefer – call it. So for anyone to say *CIVILIZATION STARTED WITH THE BLACK RACE IS WRONG. WE CREATED MANY THINGS YES BUT CIVILIZATION DID NOT START WITH US ALONE. Blacks were not the only creation of Good God. Whites resided in the Garden of Eden hence whites are found on the mountain of God.* So to the white race you can tell the Blacks to kiss your natural white ass with their repatriation bullshit bill. *What about you the whites that suffered in slavery?*

26

Who's going to pay you? Who's going to pay for your injustice? Justice does not go one way nor is it for one race. It is for all in the eyes and sight of Good God. In the Good Book of Life which is Good God's book there is justice for all hence hell is the penalty for all that sin and are unjust. Nod, Egypt, Persia, Phoenicia are the lands that must pay for repatriation and I want or need none (repatriation) from them. I don't want or need their ***BLOOD MONEY.*** They've been charged and found guilty by Life – Good God because of their lies and crimes against humanity and Good God. This is why when I see the Mountain of Good God none can be found on it.

Like I've said, the Babylonians are master liars and if the lie did not work for Evening (Eve) how the hell do you expect it to work for you today? Eve (Evening) died and you too are going to die. Humanity is slated or scheduled to die before 2032. Know that this harvest and death is for wicked and evil people – humans. Death must take his own because the time of sin is up and the majority of humans have and has signed over their life to death hence your DDC has and have been issued. (DDC is Death's Death Certificate). ***Once your DDC has and have been issued it cannot be changed. Nor will God – Good God tell death to change it. GOOD GOD***

27

HAS NOTHING TO DO WITH DEATH. HE HAS ALL TO DO WITH LIFE – GOOD LIFE.

Sin told Eve she would not die when Good God specifically told her she would die. **_She (Evening – Eve) did not listen to God – Good God, she listened to Sin and look at what it cost her?_**

You have to listen and save yourself because at the end of the day no one can die to save you from your sins. **_Did anyone die to save Eve from her sins?_** She did not listen, the people of Noah did not listen, the Israelites and Judahites did not listen and today we are not listening. Tell me something. What does it take for you to listen?

What does it take for humanity to listen?

Good God is trying to save you so truly listen man come on now.

What makes the offerings of sin so luxurious – precious that you are willing to lose it all and go to hell and burn with sin?

What makes death so precious that you are willing to die to go to hell and be a servant of death before your eventual death? You have to save you. It is your name that is on death's docket, so death must to take you. There are no

28

ands ifs or buts about this. Death must take you. Death can only be true to death. *He can only take what is given to him.* If you sin he must take you hence the wages of sin is death. So George leave the Sudanese nation alone because they did sign a pact with death. They did give up God – Good God and signed a pact with the devil hence they must go down with the devil – the Arab League. They are not God's children and because of this, I no longer want to go to South Sudan and see where life met. I am telling Good God right now that because of this, them signing over good life – their land to the devil's seed; I truly and infinitely as of this day August 05, 2013 do not want to go to South Sudan to see where life met. I refuse to step foot in that land because that land is not of you. They are the devil's own hence the pact with the death.

It's amazing how Good God has given black people – the black race good lands and we willingly sign them over to the devil to be a part of the devil's own. WHAT MAKES HELL SO GOOD THAT WE HAVE TO GO THERE (HELL) AND BE SLAVES TO THE DEVIL'S OWN – THE BABYLONIANS? WHAT MAKES DEATH SO PRETTY THAT WE HAVE

29

WANT TO LOOK LIKE DEATH AND BECOME LIKE DEATH? HELL IS THE BABYLONIANS' HOME SO LEAVE THEM ALONE.

George, leave the Sudanese people alone because the oil of the land you nor America will get. No matter the genocide of the land it must happen because they (the Sudanese) did sign their land over to the devil. ***THE PEOPLE OF SUDAN LITERALLY TOLD GOOD GOD THAT THEY ARE NOT HIS PEOPLE. THEY SPAT IN GOOD GOD'S FACE BY SIGNING A PACT WITH THE DEVIL. THEY'VE TOLD GOOD GOD THEY DON'T WANT OR NEED HIM SO LEAVE THEM ALONE.***

They must kill their people you know this.

There is no difference with what the government is doing to the people than what many of you are doing in the ELITE SATANIC CLUB OF AMERICA. Many of you have killed. Many of you have and has made your own family, friends and colleagues sacrifices unto Death – Satan.

Right now the Elite Satanic Club of America is using the black entertainers and white entertainers to do its dirty work. Every one of

30

them (the black entertainers) have killed and drank the blood of the innocent to secure a place in hell. My country is no different. 99.9 percent yes 666 of the people in dancehall and reggae today have signed a pact with Satan – Death. Hence they get the people to bleach their skin, tell people a demon dem a pree, some a floss over di dry bread – likkle 2 cents they are getting. Many kill for less because the head of the drug cartel and gun cartel lies at the head of states. Yes the members of parliament because *__for the right price you can grease a politician hand and get any child in Jamaica to sleep with. Hence Jamaica next to the Vatican – Roman Catholic Church is the pedophile and murder capital of the world. Pedophiles roam free in Jamaica. Hence a lot of young children are being raped, murdered and slaughtered like dogs and their bodies are being dumped in ditches and at the side of the road. These sickos – pedophiles are getting away with it. Trust me infinitely on this because the so-called rapists and vampires – slime and scum bags in the Jamaican Government turn a blind eye to it. But truly woe be unto them because hell will have no fury than the fury of female death.__* Death is only waiting on a couple more senseless deaths. My count has stopped because I thought death would have been unleashed already but like I said, *__HELL IS__*

31

FULL OF BLACK PEOPLE AND RECRUITING MORE. The belly of hell (the beast) is not yet full, hence the harvest is almost here and every land and people of the lands of earth must pay according to his or her works.

Every human being living and dead must pay and pay dearly because the wickedness of man has gone on for far too long.

Like I said Noah's Ark was not then it is now. Hence woe be unto man because ¼ of earth must be destroyed by fire and the other half must be destroyed by water. The reason I say this is because I saw the fire – lava ¼ the way up in the earth and water ½ the way up in the earth. Meaning the fire – lava reach ¼ the way on earth – all of earth and water reached ½ the way on earth – all of earth.

The other ¼ is reserved for Good God's true people hence they are safe and secure with Good God.

I know for a fact that fire is going to consume Jamaica but when is question. I thought it would have been sometime this summer but my three month wait period is over and nothing has happened yet. Maybe October to January of 2014. If nothing happens to Jamaica by then, then I give up. Nothing is going to happen to the

32

island then. Water destruction is easy to pinpoint but land destruction is hard – harder to pinpoint. Land destruction takes years upon years to fulfill – come. Certain destructions are quick for me. When destruction involves water they are quick but total destruction is long in coming. America is going to be destroyed this I know and now Russia is going to lay in ruin just like America hence **_USSR is done,_** The United States and Soviet Republic otherwise known as Gog and Magog. Both are going down and is going to lose it all if they don't repent. And no I am not Jonah or Noah of your book of sin.

Listen people it matters not if you hate me or not.

It matters not if you call me racist.

It matters not if you say I am going to burn in hell.

It matters not if you say I am a flake.

It matters not if you call me a fraud.

It matters not what you think of me because at the end of the day every human being – no not every human being but 99.9 % of you have your DDC which is 666 in spiritual terms. Yes the mark of the beast.

Every element of sin must die. ***So if you are a part of Satan's Elite Club you too must die. Ooh Nelly I don't want to be none of you because all of you have sold your souls for money and fame.*** Man oh man hell will be your home because in truth none of you can sell your souls to Satan because Satan hath no power in hell death does. ***DEATH IS WHAT WE ARE TO WALK BEFORE.*** Death is what we are to pass over hence the Passover. So for all you that say you sold your souls to Satan had better check yourselves because death is going to have a field day with the lots of you. You all have your DDC hence your binding contract with death. ***Oh let's not forget your children. THEY TOO HAVE THEIR DDC'S AND THEY ARE GOING TO BURN IN HELL WITH YOU.*** *I GUESS THE PERSON THAT TOLD YOU TO SIGN THE CONTRACT OF DEATH FAILED TO TELL YOU THIS PART. SO BECAUSE YOU ARE A CHILD OF DEATH, YOUR CHILDREN AUTOMATICALLY BECOMES THE CHILDREN OF DEATH – A CHILD OF DEATH. ANYTHING DEATH WANTS TO DO WITH THEM THE DEMONS OF HELL MUST CARRY OUT ON THEM (YOUR CHILDREN) INCLUDING YOU.* This is your hell. Yes your hell in the living and the spirit. ***ABSOLUTELY NOTHING YOU SAY OR DO CAN CHANGE YOUR FAITH. AND IF YOU AND YOUR CHILDREN DO NO SUFFER IN THE LIVING TRUST ME YOU WILL SUFFER IN HELL.***

34

*KNOW THAT ALL THE HEINOUS CRIMES AND ACTS THAT HUMANS DO ON EARTH, WILL BEFALL YOU AND YOUR CHILDREN IN HELL BECAUSE YOU MADE IT SO – WANTED IT SO. THIS **WILL HAPPEN TO YOU AND YOU WILL BECOME A PART OF THE ACT*** HENCE WOE BE UNTO THE LOTS OF YOU WHEN DEATH IS DONE. And yes this is why incest is so prevalent in the book of sin. Incest is hell. Acts committed in hell. Woo Nelly, I so don't want or need to be any of you. And don't think death will go against Good God because death respects Good God and truly love him. Death has a job to do and he must complete it – do it. Do you truly think death wants to take some of you vile and disgusting human beings? You pollute death and this is the reason why death has to die. Maybe one day I will write a blurb about true death and the true feel of death if Good God permits it.

You signed a pact with death and death will take you. Death will beat and destroy you in the end. HENCE THE VICTORY OF GOOD GOD AND GOD OVER SATAN, SIN, WICKED AND EVIL PEOPLE INCLUDING SPIRIT IS HELL'S FIRE. Infinitely trust me I know the fire hence I've told you what hells fire looks like. No one can say they did not know because I told you in another book. Hell is real. So for those that say it is not,

35

good luck with you in the grave. Don't want to be none of you so truly good luck to you.

Like I've said, Russia will be the first to lose their oil – resources. Many lands will, including Nodite or Babylonian lands. No one will escape this judgement. Hence whatever Earth requires of Good God, it must be granted due to our sins and the way we treat Earth – Mother Earth. We do all manner of evil in her and on her. So because of this Earth – Mother Earth can say God – Good God I want and need every human being good and evil to vacate her domain. God – Good God have to give her her desire because of our willful destruction of her.

Yes the harvest comes and humanity will feel it. This less than 19 years will be like the time of Noah, Daniel, Sodom and Gomorrah rolled up into one. This is the now generation's judgement and there is no escaping it due to sin.

We live for lies and not the truth so when death walks and take you at will do not say it is of God because GOD – GOOD GOD DID NOT TELL US TO SIN. WE WILLINGLY SINNED KNOWING FULL WELL THAT ***THE WAGES OF SIN IS DEATH.*** No one can blame Good God for the death of land and humanity. Earth must continue with the divide of lands regardless of the separation or sinking of lands with people.

36

We were told that Sodom and Gomorrah was destroyed by fire it will be so for my homeland Jamaica in this day and time. Humanity will witness this first hand because the wickedness of the people have and has reached more than the heavens.

Good God gave us good life and we are to live right, good and true. We are to respect life but many of us cannot. So George, truly look at your own nation – country because it too is slated to lose it all. Russia and his sibling the United States will lose it all and there are no ands ifs or buts about this. This will be the reality of every nation on the face of this planet.

THOU SHALT NOT KILL.

This law we all know but instead of living by this law we go against it. So because we go against the law and laws of God – Good God, we must pay the price or consequences. Every human being that is not of God – Good God must face this punishment. Billions of people are going to die and your country is no exception to this. Good God did send his messenger to tell your country how to conduct themself financially and your land (country) set him up and tarnished his image. Your government instigated a witch hunt to defame his character but **HE HAS BEEN**

37

VINDICATED BY GOOD GOD. EVERY PERSON ON THE FACE OF THIS PLANET HAVE AND HAS WATCHED AND WITNESSED THE UNITED STATES NATIONAL DEBT MORE THAN BALLOON OUT OF CONTROL – REACH 18.2 TRILLION PLUS DOLLARS. This debt is more than a sinkhole – sin that you cannot get out of. Your country rejected Good God so as your country and people rejected God – Good God Death must collapse your economy. Nations must walk away from you and let you truly fall because your national debt is more than a disgrace. Trust me when you fall you will infinitely never rise again hence God – Good God and Marcus Mosiah Garvey would have been vindicated because your nation and people rejected them.

Listen a nation of vipers cannot call another man unjust. You cannot spy on another nation by instigating war. This is what you are doing. You are causing war in a land that you know nothing about and I am asking you, Good God is asking you to truly stop

38

what you are doing. You cannot charge Sudan for genocide without charging the UNITED STATES OF AMERICA FOR GENOCIDE ALSO. YOU HAVE TO CHARGE AMERICA FOR GENOCIDE BECAUSE THEY TOO ARE GOING AGAINST GOOD GOD. Your country willingly kill for money and oil so how do you justify your homeland and what it's doing to other nations?

Good God did not tell the United States of America to act on anyone's behalf.

Good God did not tell the United States of America to kill anyone on his behalf. *HE GOOD GOD DOES NOT CONDONE ANY TYPE OF KILLING – WAR WHEN IT COMES TO HUMAN BEINGS.*

39

ALL LIFE IS PRECIOUS TO GOOD GOD BUT YET WE TAKE HUMAN LIFE WITHOUT REMORSE.

Good God never told you George Clooney to go into AFRICAN LANDS and instigate STRIFE – WAR. You are wrong.

THIS IS AFRICAN LAND AND WE DO A VERY GOOD JOB IN KILLING EACH OTHER. WE DO NOT NEED YOU ADDING MORE FUEL TO THE FIRE. You know what; in all honesty I am sick and tired of you **WHITE PEOPLE PITTING BLACKS AGAINST BLACKS. YOU DON'T KNOW US OR RESPECT US SO LEAVE US THE BLEEP ALONE. YOU'RE NOT DOING US (THE BLACK RACE) A FAVOUR BECAUSE IN TRUTH IT'S ALL A USING GAME BY YOU THE WHITE**

40

RACE. HENCE IT'S TIME BLACK PEOPLE KICK YOUR USING ASSES OFF OUR BACKS AND COAT TAILS. IF YOU HAVE NO GOOD INTENTIONS FOR BLACK PEOPLE F OFF AND LEAVE US ALONE. ENOUGH WITH YOUR SLAVERY BULLSHIT NOW MAN COME ON NOW. AND YES I AM BEING RACIST AND NO YOU CANNOT SUE ME FOR RACISM BECAUSE I AM TRULY TELLING YOU HOW I FEEL.

HOW WOULD YOU THE WHITE RACE FEEL IF THE SHOE WAS ON THE OTHER FOOT? YOU WOULD NOT LIKE IT SO STOP IT.

Murder is murder and your homeland has and have murdered Africans and Arabs – Babylonians. So tell me how is your land warranted to call themselves saints for anyone? Let me tell you something George, *you are not fooling anyone because we all know*

41

the only reason why you are in Sudan is for the oil and nothing else. If you are not, the organization that you work for is. Hence I tell God – Good God to tell Earth – Mother Earth to dry up every oil well and oil sand on earth – this planet.

True and Good Life is sacred hence no one has a right to kill or create strife.

Good God does not do it so why should man – humanity do it?

It's not Good God's fault humanity cannot live amongst each other. It's our fault because we are the ones to live for sin and do for sin.

It's not Good God's fault that we hate each other. We listened to sin. We pit each other against each other. Life is not death's sport. Life is real – good so live good come on now.

IF WE TRULY TRUSTED GOD – GOOD GOD THEN NONE OF THE BULLSHIT ON EARTH WOULD BE HAPPENING.

AS HUMANS WE FIGHT FOR A PLACE IN HELL WITHOUT KNOWING THAT WE ARE GOING TO DIE IN THE END.

GOD – GOOD GOD DID NOT CREATE DEATH, DEATH WAS BORN DUE TO OUR SINS HENCE THE WAGES OF SIN IS DEATH.

IF WE SIN NOT THEN DEATH DIES AND THIS IS THE REALITY THAT HUMAN BEINGS – HUMANITY NEED TO KNOW.

COME ON NOW. ENOUGH IS FREAKING ENOUGH.

If you want to truly help then help your country – your own but Mother Earth must yield nothing to man and if she refuses this wish – desire. If Earth refuse this wish – desire then I ask God – Good God to charge Earth – Mother Earth for treason and willful defiance of him God. I also ask Good God to take away his blessings from

43

her (earth) because she is in defiance of his law and laws. She too must be punished severely if not worse than man because she knowingly and willingly aided evil men – wicked and evil people. KNOW THIS GEORGE AND AMERICA, THE BABYLONIANS HAVE DEFEATED YOUR LAND AS WELL AS OTHER LANDS *BECAUSE THE LIKKLE DRY BREAD DEM GI UNNU A DI SAME DRY BREAD WEY KILL UNNU.* Look at the National Debt and Economy of the United States and other lands. *THE BABYLONIANS WERE SMARTER THAN YOUR ASSES HENCE THE MORE THAN SINK HOLE YOUR COUNTRY CALL THEIR NATIONAL DEBT. ABSOLUTELY NO ONE CAN DEFEAT ARIES – THE GOD OF WAR AND HIS CHILDREN ON HIS BATTLEFIELD.*

NONE!!!

NO ONE. NOT EVEN GOOD GOD BECAUSE GOOD GOD IS CLEAN NOT UNCLEAN!!!

THE BABYLONIANS NEVER WENT AGAINST THEIR GOD WHO IS DEATH. YOU AMERICA WENT AGAINST GOOD LIFE – GOOD GOD. *SIN KILL BY ANY MEANS NECESSARY HENCE THE PAY OR WAGES OF SIN IS DEATH AND AMERICA IS SLATED TO DIE MEANING BECOME BARREN.* Your people are going to starve because you take your good up good up money and fund war but more importantly SIN. Look up and you will see your national debt hence you have been defeated all around. *So, truly good luck with your land after death is done because you will never rise again.* **_Sin schooled you in the art of sin. Sin took you and your land to hell hence death comes and every man woman and child must pay for the sins of your land and the sins committed against man – other lands – nations._**

Oh Nelly when death is done with your land. You the governments put your land and people in debt, hence woe be unto you when death truly comes.

WHAT DO YOU THINK, WAR WAS THE ONLY WAY TO RUIN YOUR LAND?

REMEMBER THE DEVIL OR SATAN AS YOU CALL HIM IS THE MASTER OF DECEIT. HENCE AMERICA HAS AND HAVE BEEN DECEIVED AND THERE ISN'T A DAMN THING ANY OF YOU CAN DO ABOUT IT. YOUR LAND AND PEOPLE ARE DOOMED. SO GOOD LUCK WITH YOUR RECOVERY BECAUSE SIN – THE DEVIL WON OVER YOU HENCE YOUR CUMBLING ECONOMY AND MORE THAN A HELL HOLE OF NATIONAL DEBT. AND THIS YOU CAN THANK THE

45

BABYLONIANS FOR. BECAUSE SIN FORETOLD IT IN HIS BOOK – YOUR SO – CALLED HOLY BIBLE. HENCE, THE CODES THAT WAS EMBEDDED IN IT. AS OLD PEOPLE WOULD SAY IN MY LAND WHO NUH HEAR SHALL FEEL AND TRUST ME AMERICA IS FEELING RIGHT NOW. I WOULDN'T BE SURPRISED IF SOME OF THE STATES IN YOUR LAND SUDDENLY SINK.

SO ABAY TO AMERICA BECAUSE YOU DID NOT LISTEN TO THE MESSENGER MARCUS MOSIAH GARVEY.

HE WAS SENT BY GOOD GOD TO SAVE YOUR LAND BUT LIKE EVE AND MANY BEFORE HIM (MARCUS MOSIAH GARVEY) YOU DID NOT LISTEN AND LOOK AT THE COST TO YOU AND YOUR LAND TODAY. <u>YOU FAILED GOOD GOD. GOOD GOD DID NOT FAIL YOUR PEOPLE AND LAND.</u>

REMEMBER THE NAME:

<u>MARCUS MOSIAH GARVEY</u>

He did try to help you and he did foretell. Good God did send him to you and you did refuse him. Just check your records of what you America did to him. My land also failed him hence the people of my homeland must truly

46

deal with Good God and what they did to his messenger – Marcus Mosiah Garvey as well. ***__Woe be unto Jamaica hence their sink hole of a national debt is in line with yours except theirs is in the billions not trillions. America has 18.2 trillion+ in debt and Jamaica has 18.2 billion+ in debt.__*** There is no difference in number except for the value.

Enough is enough. And if Good God does not grant me this petition of goodness I will truly go against him in the end but I can't. I would be overstepping my boundaries so scrap that.

You cannot willingly kill others for oil because the oil of the land does not belong to any human. It belongs to Earth – Mother Earth. We are the ones to steal it and sell it. We as human beings are the thieves of the land and trust me many lands will pay for robbing Mother Earth of her natural resources. Good God gave us none of her resources to steal so why take her resources without permission?

__Tell me something can a man make dirt – the dirt of the land – earth grow?__

No for real can he or she?

No right?

__So how the hell can a man take that which he cannot produce – make – create?__

__Can a man take water air and dirt and create a human just like that?__

__So how the hell can a man or woman say he or she can create?__

Earth is a source of life and when we take all life from earth – Mother Earth what do we have left? What we take from the earth we are to replenish it's that simple.

No, I am not speaking for Sudan on this day because Sudan signed a pact with the devil. They withdrew themselves from Good God and gave death the Blue and White Nile – the joining of Life and for this I truly hope Good God never forgive them.

__Someone tell me why is it that Good God gave us the black nations GOOD LIFE AND WE WILLINGLY GIVE IT UP TO BE AMONGST THE DEVIL'S OWN. HAVE WE NOT LEARNT FROM EVE (EVENING) AND WHAT SHE DID?__

She gave up life for the devil and we are still doing it until this day. We say we are Africans but yet as Africans we disgrace God and make him hold his head down in shame and disgrace. Now you have blacks bleaching their skin to look ugly like sin. Sin is ugly that is why sin have to wear makeup to hide its ugliness. Sin's stink that's why sin have to wear so much perfume to mask his stinkiness. Man some of you bathe in perfume that in some doctors office they have to put up signs to tell you to tone it down on the perfume use because it's too strong.

So with all of this happening, why should Good God stay with any of us?

We've proven to God – Good God we do not deserve him. Hence I tell you sin's greatest weapon against Good God is humanity – humans.

We say Satan tempted Jesus on the mount by offering him everything but because Jesus did not exist and no one can dispute these words. ___It is humanity that sin tempted and___

49

<u>offered all to and humanity has and have accepted the offerings of sin. We failed God and Self. Humans – humanity are going to die a brutal death and no one can blame Good God for this, we can only blame self. We are the ones to accept the offerings of sin knowing full well that we are going to die.</u>

So George, know what you are doing because all that you do you are not aiding Africa or a African Nation you are aiding the devil and his nation of demons because they excluded themselves from Africa. Sudan is not united with Good God and Africa. They are united with death – the Arabs otherwise known as Babylonians. What are you telling Good God and Me? Are saying you are against him (Good God) and that you are united with SIN?

Do you truly think these people are with you? Please. ***One is in America training Black Americans to fight against your asses.*** This will be the beginning of their Holy Jihad – War. ***Hence I tell every black*** *person around the globe that this Babylonian DEMON has converted to Islam to stand down.*

Do not go against Good God for this demon because he did not tell you that his homeland sold out Good God long ago to accept the devils' own.

You cannot fight for Sudan or any Arab nation because Babylon – Nod – their lying and thieving ancestors **COLONIZED OUR ASSES LONG BEFORE THE EUROPEANS.**

THEY STOLE OUR LANDS AND BIRTHRIGHT AND GAVE US THEIR STINKING AND NASTY GODS AND RELIGIONS TO WORSHIP. All that is evil and sinful they gave to us to defile ourselves, land and god. Hence we defile Good God.

Look at it, they take off their shoes to worship but yet you can't. Good God's children had respect for Good God and now we don't.

51

Good God's children had the respect of him and now we don't. He can't even look upon us due to the vile and abominable sins we commit.

Instead of listening to Good God we listened to them and now Good God is not with us. He's left man.

Now we are scrambling to find him and can't.

Onwards I go

This man who claims to be re-incarnated of the four and twenty elders is a FRAUD THAT IS TAKING YOUR SOULS TO HELL. URDU IS THE MOTHER TONGUE OF ARABIC. LOOK AT THE LANGUAGE AND SEE FOR YOURSELVES.

India is the original land of Nod – the name was just changed to fool your asses. This is why some Muslims tell you to change your name to reflect the devils name which is Ali, Abram, Abraham, Mohammed, Singh, Sing, Singer you name it. Like I've told you, **IF THE LIE DID NOT WORK FOR EVE HOW THE HELL IS IT GOING TO WORK FOR YOU?**

52

Any one of you that have and has changed your name to reflect any of these names have and has accepted sin – death. If your name is not Singh, Sing, Mohammed, Ali and you change your name to reflect any of these names you have committed an abominable sin. You've committed a grave lie – sin *and you have caused any children born unto you to become a lie and a sin in the eyes and sight of Good God and man.* There is no forgiveness for this. I've told you you have a chance in the living to change this. You have one chance to change your child's name to the truth. ***If you die and do not change this (wrong name) then you will not see Good God nor will your child see Good God. You would have committed an abominable sin as well as caused your child to live in sin. You and your child will go to hell and burn because you both died living in a lie. Good God does not like lies hence, "TRUTH IS EVERLASTING LIFE." No lie can enter Good God's abode because lies are sins punishable by death. We all know this so truly do better.*** Yu sinned, caused your child to be born in sin and die in sin. Yes I said you cannot change your birth certificate but you have a chance in the living to correct your wrong. Take it and don't look back. You cannot change your original sin but you can correct it. Meaning make amends for the wrong you have done.

53

Remember your child was born right but YOU MADE YOUR CHILD WRONG BY REGISTERING HIM OR HER WRONG. No lie can see Good God. If you are a liar in the living you are still a liar in death. Death cannot change your lies he can only keep them. I hope I explained that correctly for you to comprehend.

If you do not know the name of your child's father then it's permissible to give your child your last name. But you cannot under any circumstances give him or her another man's name. If you do this you must pay and will pay. And no it matters not if you've adopted a child. You cannot change his or her birth certificate to reflect your name. Your adopted child's birth certificate must stay as is. And yes it is permissible for your adopted child to give his children your name in honour of you. He or she cannot give their children your last name as a surname it must be his own. The adopted name must come before the surname. For example, if your child was born Brown and your name is say Johnson. He must keep Brown as a last name. However he can do this in honour of you. Give his child a name like Dayna Johnson Brown or Dayna Johnson-Brown or Johnson Dayna Brown. Johnson is in remembrance of you and your family hence the family name at the beginning or before the surname. And no Good God will not charge your child for sin

54

because a good last name including first name is a blessing in the eyes and sight of Good God. This cannot change and yes a child can divorce their biological parents hence adoption in many cases. When he or she can divorce parents they cannot divorce their names – sir name.

If your parents are dead you cannot change your name. You will die wrong and you can thank your parents for that. You cannot right their wrong. *(Do not quote me on this. When I get further confirmation I will let you know. So if you know your parents gave you the wrong name at birth and they have died petition Good God and ask about this meaning changing your correct name to the right name. You cannot right them (your parents) but you can right you. Know that Good God is the knower and fixer of all.)*

What if one parent is dead and the other is alive you are saying? The person that registered you is the person that must correct you and in many cases it's the mother that registered you. Do not give up, still petition God and tell him your circumstances. Good God will find a way for you meaning help you in the course of action you need to take.

If a man refuses to accept his child as his own, then register your child in your name. Do not give that child another man's name. Exclude the man if he wants to be excluded. You be the mother and father for your child. Trust me Good God will truly provide for you if you let him.

Also, make sure your child know who his or her father is. Infinitely know this, any man or woman that do not own up to his or her responsibility as a parent (mother and father) is truly dead to God – Good God. None, not one will see him or enter into his kingdom – abode. There are no ands ifs or buts about this. This is the law of Good God because children are a blessing to humanity – life due to good and true birth.

I know some of you are saying I can't take care of my child and I have him her up for adoption.

Know this, ***you did nothing wrong.*** You are providing for your child by giving him or her a good home. Good God will never judge you or charge you for sin on this. It is better to give your child a good home where he or she can grow good rather than to leave him or her in misery. No exchange of money should be involved in the adoption process but because of the way man's legal system is set up it cannot be helped.

Further, any man or woman including clergy that tells you to live in a lie – sin is truly dead to Good God. Do right and good and right and good will be with you always. Yes right and good will follow you.

No one should tell you to accept a family name that is incorrect. The family that you are born unto is your family name as well as your birthright. So don't give away your birthright like many so-called AFRICAN NATIONS. Also, let no one steal your birthright. ***YOUR BIRTHRIGHT IS YOU GOD GIVEN RIGHT AND ENTITLEMENT.*** If your family name is Johnson you cannot register your child Ali or Mohammed. You are lying to God and Man and this is wrong – a sin and you will go to hell and die for this.

So to all the Black American's that are going the Islamic way think again because the

57

Babylonians were the first ones to enslave and beat our asses. *We gave up our lives for them and look at Africa today. More importantly look at all the lands that were colonized and given Arabic – the language of death. Hence the bible talked about Nimrod and the different languages of the Babylonians.* They Babel, hence the tower of Babel in Nimrod's time – the Babylonian era. They said God scattered them. Good God did not scatter them because God – Good God hath nothing to do with sin and his people. And no, the devil did not go on no mount to tempt Jesus. Bullshit because Good God would never send his children into the lion's den to save the children of sin – death. God – Good God would infinitely never ever send his children to die for sins children. Sins children belong to death hence the domain of death which is hell belongs to them. It is a fool that thinks someone is going to come into the grave or come out of the sky to save them.

WE WILLINGLY SIN HENCE WE ARE ACCOUNTABLE FOR OUR SINS. If you go to Revelations One (1) you will get the description of Jesus and I am telling you this.

NO BLACK MAN OR WOMAN IN HIS OR HER RIGHT MIND WOULD GO AGAINST

58

GOOD GOD AND DIE FOR DEATH'S CHILDREN.

Come on now. Which child of Good God would give up their good up, good up place and home with him to save some of your racist asses? *Which one of us would sacrifice self for any one of you? I certainly wouldn't.* I would tell greater death to increase the fire from 1 billion degrees to 21 trillion+ degrees Centigrade. Hell no when it comes to saving death's children. *The nerve of them saying God – Good God would kill his own child to save them.* **Who are they anyway?** Your god kills hence there is hell. Come on now. Why should one man die for all of humanity? Please. Humanity isn't worth it. You sinned and someone is to take the place of you and burn in hell while you go to God's abode and live nice – good? One individual is to go to hell and take the ridicule and beatings of the demons of hell and you go free. **Tell me now, what do you take God – Good God for?**

Do you think Good God is an idiot? Come on now. You are living fine and dandy with God – Good God. This man or person did nothing, but yet he's to die for you, burn for you, live in misery for you? This person truly did not love life or Good God.

59

He truly hated himself because there is no way in hell I would give myself over to death to be enslaved, beaten and burned for anyone. Come on now. I didn't even mention the rest of the horrible things the demons of hell are going to do to him. Trust me not even Good God I would die for and I truly and infinitely truly love him. Come on now.

No. Death is not worth it. So why should I die to see death hence the lies about Jesus and the story of Jesus. God's so-called son died and all of evil's children lived. Come on now. God - Good God is no fool so wake up to the truth. Humanity is the fool because we believe crap and say they are from Good God. When did Good God and his children become the scapegoat of death? Oh yea I forgot, we made God the Sabbath hence the Sabbath Goat of Death. Sorry God – Good God because humanity has and have turned you into a fool. Hence they say Sabbath – made you their scapegoat that they trample down on their Sabbath Day – DAY OF DEATH.

So George, truly know what you are doing when it comes to Sudan because you truly don't know the holy jihad that is waiting for your ass.

No one can spy on you. Now I say this without regret.

If war breaks out in Sudan everyone in humanity can say you are the cause of it because you stuck your nose in where it did not belong.

You are doing nothing GOOD for Sudan because the oil is the main goal and you will never have it. It is not permitted nor will it be permitted. *You say you are using your own money to fund your perverted campaign – your spy campaign.* ***How dare you do this? This is not America this is Africa. There is a big difference. Black people have been raped enough for you to intrude on their privacy.***

Black people have been raped enough for you to instigate war between two brothers. Enough is enough.

Take a good look at you – self. You claim the paparazzi of the United States are intrusive but yet you intrude on another man's privacy. ***Well bleep you because it's only sick perverts and stalkers that watch people.*** Don't tell me you are one of those people that like to .... never mind you are because you spy on *BLACK PEOPLE IN THEIR OWN HOME LANDS. Tell me*

61

something, do you get pleasure out of seeing BLACK PEOPLE BEFORE YOU? What should they do now? Should they undress so that you can get a further kick – high? Better yet why don't you........ no, soon they will be in one of your lame ass movies that spread propaganda while you swoop in on your fake ass white horse of death saying you're the saviour for the Black Race. Since you like to spy on the Black Race so much, maybe all the paparazzi of the world should turn their cameras on you and spy on your ass since you like spying so much.

Spying is not the answer.

War is not the answer.

So stop invading Black People's privacy. **_Can anyone from Sudan come to America and spy on your ass?_**

Can Sudan spy on America with these cameras without America being up in arms and wanting to wipe all Sudanese off the planet with your warring mentality?

Sudan is not America and Good God did not give you AMERICAN WAR GAMES to play with the lives of Sudanese people.

You want to spy on people, join your damned President and spy on your own not on Sudan. He too should be ashamed because he is of African lineage and he infinitely do not represent Africa and Africans. Goes to show you when Good God gives us power, meaning ordain us to do his good works we turn against him.

Know this Sudan. If you don't change from the Babylonian Way and repent of your sins then truly good luck to you this harvest because another black land will bite the dust literally.

ARABS DON'T LIKE BLACK PEOPLE PERIOD.

THEY ARE NOT FING BLACK. THEY ARE THE DEMON SEEDS OF HELL. So why the hell are BLACK NATIONS KISSING THEIR ASSES AND MINGLING WITH THEM?

Their way is of the devil hence no Muslim is found in the abode of Good God. *Islam is what Good God is trying to save Africa and his people from but yet Africans refuse to listen.* **_LIKE I SAID, GOOD GOD CANNOT TRUST US BECAUSE WE CONSTANTLY SELL HIM OUT TO BE APART OF THE DEVIL'S OWN._**

You George cannot stay the death of Sudan. Sudan chose death over life hence they are a part of the Arab league – the league of death.

63

Also, since you have so much money to spend on invading the privacy and rights of black people, why don't you petition your government to cut their war fund and spend some of that almost 1 trillion dollars they spend to kill and make weapons on bringing down their sinkhole of a hell hole they call the National Debt?

Why don't you use your *BLOOD MONEY* that you are using to invade the privacy of black people and help pay down your countries sink hole and stink hole of a national debt? Right is right and wrong is wrong and you George Clooney is infinitely wrong. Jamaican's would say what you don't know olda dan yu. ***So truly be mindful of the devil that is standing at your door step.*** George, I truly love you but you need to think and do right. ***If a man is bent on sacrificing his land and people to death you cannot change him nor can you stop him.***

Both sides of the fence have a pact with death. They have to walk away from death's door on their own. ***THE WAR BETWEEN NORTH AND SOUTH WILL NEVER STOP. SIN AND DEATH MUST BE LOCKED UP IN HELL'S FIRE; BOUND WITH THE KEY AND SWORD OF DEATH BEFORE THE FIGHTING STOPS. THIS IS WHAT THIS HARVEST IS FOR. EVERY LAND THAT IS NOT OF GOOD GOD MUST SUFFER – BE DEVOURED.***

Sin's time is up hence death comes to collect his offerings – his sin offering – that which sin has and have given him and that his humanity.

If you are not of Good God then death must take you so leave these people alone. Further, I am asking every Black Muslim to rethink what they are doing. Like I said, you cannot go against Good God for the Babylonians. They lied to Eve and she did die and you will die also. This man is lying to you because he too is a Babylonian that Babel – speak the tongue of Nimrod which is his ancestor. Go back to Babylon – Babel and see what Nimrod did to his people. You are no exception to this slavery when the Babylonians take control. And if any of you think that Good God is going to stand with you or rescue you, truly think again. You will be like the people of Noah. Truly dead in the eyes and sight of Good God hence none were saved. You will be infinitely dead to him because you would have helped the Babylonians to take down your own. Do not be like the Judas's of my homeland that sold out Good God. You are being warned. America is your home and no matter the state of disarray it is in. It is your home of birth – birthright. We the black race are not innocent because we did sell our own long before the Europeans came along. Go back to Genesis and see what Eve did. She let evil into Good God's kingdom. ***Correct her mistake and***

live. *Do not follow a Black Devil and destroy your land. Do not follow this Black Devil to your deaths because what he is teaching you is wrong – false. One thing he forgot to tell all of you is that Islam is a spiritual prison and if you die a Muslim you will be trapped for all eternity in a spiritual prison. There will be no escape for you. So truly think. Good God has been trying with us for centuries. We are the ones to refuse him. If we refuse him now then there will be no saving grace for you and your children.*

None of us came from slaves, our own made us slaves in the living and in death. *Come on now Allelujah. Come on now man listen and learn the truth.* **IT'S TIME THE BLACK RACE STOP SELLING OUT SELF AND GOOD GOD. COME ON NOW.**

THOU SHALT NOT KILL hence I am telling you in the name of good God – Allelujah to stand down. *Do not pick up arms against America. If you do you will be charged for treason in the eyes of Good God. Trust me you will never ever, infinitely never see him. Whether you like it or not, God – Good God gave the United States of America good life meaning the upright triangle with the eye in it.* **This demon is trying to take that from you. You have spiritual life – good life so live by good life. Come on now.** Islam is a spiritual prison and no child of God – Good

66

God must associate themselves with the devil's clan. Eve (Evening) married one and it did cost her her life and place with him. ***Sudan is not an African Nation by proxy.*** Don't even say it because I know the you idiot thing. ***Sudan signed an agreement to be a part of the Arab Nation. They did not sign the agreement to stay with Africa. So because of this they cannot call themselves Africans. They must call themselves Arabs – Babylonians. They gave up God – Good God to become the devils clowns so you have to leave them alone.***

Like I said, we as blacks have and has disgraced Good God and self long enough and it's time we know our true history including heritage. God – Good God has and have been protecting us from the fire – the Babylonians and we keep running into the fire. We keep rejecting Good God and it's time for this to stop. ***We cannot let lying Babylonians including Black Babylonians – Black Death lie to us anymore.***

America was once a part of Africa but that land broke away. The cycle of separating good from evil did not complete hence you will see many lands separate. The separation of good lands from evil lands must be in this day and time hence the water is ½ way.

EVERY LAND OF GOD – GOOD GOD HOUSES THE TRUTH and America is no different.

America houses the truth and that truth is the ***EYE IN THE UPRIGHT TRIANGLE like I've said before.*** It is on your dollar bill, plus you say in God we trust. Hence I ask, which God do you trust? There is the God of Life and the God of Death hence life and death, so which God do you truly trust America?

If you say life, then I ask you this. Why do you spend over 700 billion on death – war each year? You do not trust Life you trust death – Aries the god of war.

Life cannot kill. Death kills hence you spend your money on death – the willful murdering of other people. ***YOU AMERICA GAVE UP LIFE. JUST LIKE ALL OTHER BLACK NATIONS THAT GOOD GOD TRUSTED WITH HIS LIFE, NAME AND WELL BEING. YOU TOO HAVE DISGRACED GOOD GOD. YOU TOO HAVE WALKED AWAY FROM GOOD GOD. YOU TOO HAVE ACCEPTED THE DEVIL'S OWN AS YOUR OWN*** hence the harvest comes for you also. Like

68

I've said, your land will be held accountable along with the people of your land because greater disasters are yet to come for you and your people. Good God tried to save your land and you refused him. You rejected Good God and his messenger and look what it cost you. A 18.2 trillion dollar+ sink and stink hole that you caused upon yourself. *I would love to say your 18.2 trillion dollar sink and stink hole can fill up all the man made sink holes of this earth but I cannot due to the width of these holes.* **Your debt to death is massive so good luck with that – trying to pay it down. <u>AMERICA YOU OWE DEATH BIG TIME.</u>** So to the people of America, you can thank your inept government for this massive debt. And none of you dear blame your current President Barak Obama. He inherited your sink hole so try to help him bring your national debt down. So for you racist asses that say a black man should not be president of the United States. Go back to the hell hole you crawled out of literally because he Barack represents Africa. With him (Barak) being President just means Africa came full circle with the Ying and Yang because he is of mixed linage hence Kenya and the spear of death. Put it together if you can. (A black man took the white house people). (Black Death is sitting in the House of Death hence Black and White Death came together on a different level – the political level). Now truly put it together. ***He Barack was***

69

to bring stability to your country because America is not fully gone. Renewable Energy is the key to humanities sustainability.

So Barak truly cut your military spending (the spending of death) and use some of that money to pay down your national debt. Good God ordained you whether you know it or not. (Just look into the Kenyan lineage because neither you nor your people knoweth the truth and greatness of Kenya. Your father's homeland is that old – blessed. Just look at the coat of arms because as simple as the spear looks it is the spear of death. That which kills Satan's children in the spiritual realm). So truly kill death as you were ordained to do. Cut your military spending and save your land and people. This is your job so do it in the name of God – Good God. Dethrone death and let your land and people live.

You had to win because it was ordained.

Further, it matters not what people say. It matters not the association with the wrong kind – lodge man. I am telling you you were ordained to win. This was not the doing of anyone on earth but the doing of Good God because I saw

70

it. Evil will tell you they did but I am telling you God – Good God did. Nothing the devil did could have hindered you. Trust me infinitely you were ordained to take office. There are no ands ifs or buts about this so represent Good God and bring your country's national debt down. Lead by Good God's example because you were chosen. Make a difference to Good God because God is trying to save your land. Not because of anything good America has done but because of the eye in the triangle. Many associate this with the Eye of Horus but this is a great injustice unto GOOD LIFE – GOOD GOD. The eye in the triangle has nothing, infinitely nothing to do with Horus – a Babylonian deity. It has to do with Life – Good Life so know this. God gave your land good life to keep and nourish and you are throwing it away foolishly. You have life – good life so represent good life come on now. The triangle is significant to life and death hence the Ying and Yang. They are both the same Male and Female hence the representation of God – Good God. The oil that the world is fighting for is going to be gone. Like I said, Russia is the first nation to lose it. Do not ask me why. I can only relate what I saw so Russia had better smarten up because it will all come together with the Baltic Sea for some strange reason but do not quote me on this. Something is to happen in that region but I cannot fully say because I truly do not know. I do not know if it is war but

71

something is to happen so Russia better take heed and leave the Babylonians alone. They too are being warned hence this book and if they do not listen they will lose it all in the same manner as you America. Remember America has two strikes against them. Meaning you refused Martin Luther King Jr. and Marcus Mosiah Garvey. One more strike and you will be infinitely and indefinitely gone. ***ABSOLUTELY NOTHING WILL SAVE YOU.*** *So listen and cut the spending of death because death comes to collect the pay of sin. Sin offered humanity as an offering and now death wants it hence the harvest that is coming. Death must and will collect his pay hence many lands will be left barren – without food and water.* ***America can save self so do it now. Do not wait until the LAST NANO SECOND OR YOU WILL BE TOO LATE.***

America grows sugarcane, corn, wheat; barley you name it you grown it. So let these products work for you in regards to fuel alternatives.

Jamaica grows sugarcane, beets, cassava, vegetables. Encourage them to grow more of these produce and buy from them. They also need to save their economy so truly help them to do this in the name of God – Good God.

Your eyes represent Life – the sight of God depending on the direction of your triangle which is Life itself. Your country represents good life but you are not acting good, you are acting bad. Hence your land **does not represent good life it represents death and this is why your land is getting a beating.** You accepted the eye in the triangle – the upright triangle with the eye and you lie to people by abusing life – killing. You cannot say your land is of God and have such a massive debt.

Good God owes no one so why does your land owe everyone including death?

Your beatings will not stop because you go against life. The upright triangle with the eye represents good life and the ascension of good life up to God – Good God. Like I said, this has nothing to do with Babylonian deities. ***And like I said and will forever say, the Babylonians seek importance when they hath none. They are not a part of God's plan – the mountain of Good God hence they steal the truth of God's people and pollute it with their nasty and filthy selves.*** Not one of them can be found on the mountain of Good God hence Moses went up the mountain; Martin Luther King Jr. saw the mountain and I've seen the mountain but

73

went up the wrong mountain in reality literally. The Mountain is significant to Good God because the mountain in one way is the gateway and home of Good God. Not all Mountains but one specific mountain and that is the Blue Mountain. So any land on the face of this planet that houses a Blue Mountain houses the truth and home of Good God on a physical and spiritual level. Blue is a significant and powerful colour in the spiritual realm people and this is why I say the Blue Mountain houses the truth and home of Good God on a physical and spiritual level. You America house the truth of life – good life like I said and you abuse it – destroy it. So as you destroy Good God and Life your land too will be destroyed – become desolate and this is what's happening today with the tornadoes, hurricanes and fires. You need to learn that you have the true key to life and you cannot disrespect your good and true life by fighting for the devils own. Goodness is within your land, so stick to the goodness Good God has given you. Walk away from the devil now and repent of your sins. ***Good God truly want to save your land and I so don't know why and God – Good God truly forgive me for making that statement.*** I know that land houses life hence I will not bash you for the decision you have made in regards to them. So to all that keep bashing the upright triangle with eye don't. *And stop associating it with death* *because it is not death but true life.* **YOUR SYMBOL REPRESENT LIFE AND NO OTHER LAND HAS IT EXCEPT ISRAEL FOR WHICH YOU CALL EGYPT.** Yes it's kind of awkward calling Egypt Israel but facts are facts. Yes other lands houses the upright triangle but your symbol has more significance from a life standpoint. Meaning the paper it is written or printed on. ***Writings are important to Good God so do not continue to go against your truth.*** Man cannot destroy the eye in the upright triangle hence Babylon tires to destroy you by other means.

YOUR NATIONAL DEBT IS ONE OF THEM.

The fighting with evil (the Babylonians) is another.

Like I said, no one can defeat Aries – the God of War on his battlefield because war is not the only means to bring humanity to their knees – cause us to die.

Our sins cause us to die.

The lies we tell cause us to die.

The adultery we do cause us to die.

The death we believe in and accept cause us to die.

The death we marry in cause us to die.

Sin has us locked but we can free ourselves hence the clean life that we should and must live daily.

Remember the law which states, ***"THOU SHALT NOT KILL."*** So stop playing the games of the Babylonians. Stop killing and guard your economy because shortly ***the banks of the world will complete the final fall and that is to transfer the wealth of the people of your lands to Nod,*** so truly protect yourself.

Go back to the beginning of the book of sin. Eve did fall – die. Hence all she was promised by sin she never got. (And yes this is why many say, "A promise is a comfort to a fool").

She did not listen to the good advice and counsel of Good God and she died three times hence the THREE DAUGHTERS OF DEATH THAT WALK IN UNISON.

The book of sin referred to them as Cain, Seth and Abel the three sons of Eve but in truth ***they were the three deaths of Eve (Evening).*** Now you infinitely and truthfully know the full truth.

76

Let no one tell you otherwise because you have been given the full truth of the beginning. Satan never fell from grace because Satan hath no grace. ***Eve (Evening fell from grace because she was with Good God.*** He Satan was not a child of Good God Eve (Evening) was. *Sin and his people are giver backer takers.*

Listen to Good God and you will not go wrong or be wrong.

When this transfer (the transfer of humanities wealth) is done, then Babylon would have won.

The devil would have defeated man and revelations would be complete. *Hence good lands must now separate their good banking systems from evil's banking system so that they are not caught up with death in this harvest that is to come.* And don't even think Canada hence read further. If I do not get to Canada think of the moon I told you about in another book. *The white yellow and gold moon – the colours of the African Unity Flag – the flag of death.*

Africa when you raise the unity flag you are raising the flag of death hence take the green out. You cannot raise the white and blue flag but you can raise the white

77

and yellow flag. This represent power – spiritual power so clean up your act – lands and change your colours and become clean. You can keep the tree of life – wreath because the wreath represents the leaf of life – trees.

Know that **the Ying and Yang is what you need to know not just in the grave but in life.** Truly know this. If you see an inverted triangle with the eye in it, it means your home is hell when you die. If you see an upright triangle with the eye in it, it means your home is with God – Good God. So America this is what your eye in the triangle means. It means you are going to live with Good God because you have it on paper. *But as it is, you are not going to live with Good God because you desecrate life – take life hence your sink hole of a national debt. You also lied to Good God because you do not protect the eye in upward triangle nor do you keep it clean.*

You cannot say you trust God and go against his law and laws. Hence I say every land of God disrespect him. We've all forgotten the significance of life and this is sad. Every land of God has and have turned from his goodness to follow the sins of the devil without knowing that

78

the devil or sin has and have handed them over to death.

We disgrace God – Good God so much that I truly have to wonder why he tries with us. Oh well we pay to learn and will forever pay to learn if we do not smarten up. And as for you, you so called devil worshippers and Satan lovers you do not worship Satan you worship death and live for death. **_You all have your DDC'S hence your children have them also. Your children are going to burn and die alongside you in hell._**

So George, truly help your country because at the end of the day God can truly charge you for sin because you are going against life. *I know you are trying to do good and I commend you for that* **BUT DO GOOD FOR YOUR OWN FIRST BEFORE YOU EXTEND THE OLIVE BRANCH OF TRUTH TO PEOPLE THAT HAVE SOLD OUT GOOD GOD LITERALLY. YES, LIFE CAME TOGETHER IN THEIR LAND BUT YOUR HOMELAND HAVE THE TRUE GIFT OF LIFE SO TRULY SAVE YOUR OWN. _At the end of the day your own need help so do good and well by America – Americans. Once again, I truly thank you for what you are trying to do but do not lose sight of America. At the end of the day, the oil that man fight and kill for will be gone. Russia will be the first to cast nets – hoses and literally yield_**

nothing. No oil will be there for them. It's not just Russia that will yield nothing every land on earth that is not of Good God will yield nothing. The sins of man has and have reached the heavens. Beyond the heavens, hence the harvest comes and humanity will suffer and suffer severely. Trust me every pain and suffering that death can unleash on man will be unleashed. Hence death is going to empty his cup on man and real soon. I am looking towards 1313 which I say is December 2013. I could be wrong but I am hoping that I am not wrong when it comes to the date. Physical time must catch up to spiritual time ***hence to me*** December 2013 is when this will happen and we will see the beginning of the downfall of humanity – man and their evil system of things.

Humanity can change this hence but it's up to each and every human being on the face of the planet. We know evil has no respect of person and I keep asking, if we know that we are going to go to hell and burn why live to die? Why not live to live come on now.

It's beyond me why anyone would give up their life to go to hell and burn hotter than a bitch. Like I said, if we cannot cope with the heat of earth during the summer, how the hell are we going to cope in hell?

HELL HATH NO AIR CONDITIONERS OR SNOW

so why want to go there? Why live your life for sin?

The harvest comes now and if the United States and Russia do not change then humanity can write these two countries off the map of Good God literally.

Hell and sin is not worth it.

1.3 billion is slated to die of incurable cancer so what say humanity? I say slated to die. *But this 1.3 billion could be all that have died since man created the disease cancer to kill the human population. (The 6th sign of the zodiac – Virgo. Now put it together if you can).* And no one better say well God created Cancer when he created humans. No human being that Good God created had any form of disease. ***And for the record Good God did not create man – humans we came about though the fusion of water – which is the union of the egg and sperm through the collaboration of heat and cold (sun and moon) to generate the right atmosphere – temperature for this union to take place.***

Good God didn't make diseases humans did. Good God did not mess with the genetics of

81

humans, humans did and we are still doing until this day. God – Good God do not want or need a perfect race of people, wicked and evil people do hence humans do. Good God gave us everything perfect, we as humans are the ones to make things imperfect. Good God made everything on the face of the planet good and true. We as humans are the ones to want more and more because of greed. We are the ones to live for greed.

Sin comes and offers his dirty contracts – deals of death to kill humanity and we accept it hence losing our place with Life – Good God. We fell for the traps and lies of sin and in doing so we forgot about God – Good God. ***Sin gave us all but in all sin did for man, sin was bringing humanity to shame and disgrace – his or her knees – inevitable death.***

All that is happening to humanity is not Good God's doing but death's doing. DEATH MUST GET PAID AND THE PAY OF DEATH IS OUR SINS HENCE WE DIE A HORRIBLE AND BRUTAL DEATH TODAY.

No one had to die but we accepted sin without thinking of the consequences to us – humanity on a whole.

82

Like I said, **_we can change the course of this harvest if we are good but if you are wicked and evil you cannot. You must go with death. If you are wicked and evil you cannot pass over death (the Passover) because you lived for evil as well as gave your soul over to death – evil._**

As for you Christians that say you will be saved you had infinitely better think again because God – Good God has more than a bone to pick with the lots of you. No Jesus will save you because Jesus did not exist. No one on the face of this planet can prove that Jesus existed and no, you cannot use Zeus to prove your point. And don't say oh either. Forget it, Nimrod and his mother won't work either. Baal and Balaam don't work either. Forget it because Melchesidec does not work either. Even if you refute me, you infinitely and indefinitely cannot prove me wrong. Hence no one can prove God – Good God wrong. And don't even think it because I am not classing myself as God – Good God, so don't even go there. I know the lots of you hence I truly and infinitely have God – Good God. Even if you continue to say, Jesus exist, God – Good God will never look upon any of you because you disrespect Good God worse than a It (Transgender) Thing. By walking in your churches – churches you say is of God – Good God with your filthy and dirty shoes you are

83

showing and telling Good God that you don't respect him – **_HATH NO RESPECT FOR HIM LITERALLY._** Hence you wear your nasty shoes in churches.

See the Babylonians tell you it's okay but if it was okay why are they shoeless in their Mosques? Did not the book of sin say Moses, Moses take off thy shoe because the place you are standing on is holy ground? So if your churches were holy ground why are your dirty shoes still on your feet?

So because you disrespect and disgrace Good God your names are not written in Good God's book of Life. **_This disrespect is what the Ethiopians did to God – Good God and God hates them that they are no longer a part of Good God's kingdom. No Ethiopian can be found in God's abode hence God – Good God do not look upon them or see them._** And like I said before Good God does not hate. I asked the question why does God hate the Ethiopians and was shown the answer. And the reason why I used the word hate was because I read it somewhere that God hated the Ethiopians.

I was shown the answer like I said. So if God truly hates them, what say you that do the same to Good God as the Ethiopians today?

No one can sin to see God that is a known fact. So why do we continue to shut ourselves out of Good God's kingdom by following the Babylonians nasty and sinful way of doing things?

Why do you continue to sin knowing that Good God does not like it?

Clean yourself up now man come on now. And Barack your pettiness is not warranted because as a President ***YOU SHOULD KNOW THAT WHAT'S DONE IN THE DARK MUST COME TO LIGHT ONE DAY.*** So what if you listen on peoples conversation. Some people get a high off you listening to them so ***MOVE ON.*** Technology ***WAS DESIGNED TO BE INTRUSIVE.*** So get over your pettiness and truly move on because *the majority of the population on earth has nothing to hide.* Trust me, listening in on my conversation makes me feel important because it will give people something to talk about. ***And don't you dare listen in on my conversation. This is not a ticket to say listen to me. I truly do love my privacy.***

By you harbouring bad feelings for the Vladimir Putin does not say much for your character nor does it say much for Vladimir Putin if he harbours bad feelings for you. Do not talk about Russia violating the rights of their citizens. ***Pick***

85

__the beam out of the eye of the United States of America before you pick it out of the next man and country.__ America does not treat the **__BLACKS of the land good or fair.__** A prime example of this was the assassination of Martin Luther King Jr., the defamation of Marcus Mosiah Garvey's character by the United States Government and more recently the willful murder of Trayvon Martin. *No one in their right mind can condone this grave miscarriage of justice but yet blacks are faced with this each and every day in your country.* *Your National Debt also speaks volumes for itself as to how your land has raped your children and the future of all American children of a future.* You spend more on war but yet people in your land go homeless and hungry. Stop the petty games because it does not become you.

As for you Vladimir Putin you are no better. You and Barack are acting like children and not even children are this childish. This is not a snobby chess game; this is reality so grow up. Your land (Russia) is no better than America when it comes to injustice and miscarriage of justice. Human beings including your people have all the right to call you a a-hole or a dick and Nimrod if they feel you are this. Bullying your nation – people into submission goes against their God given rights. **__You are willingly taking their rights and freedom away from__**

86

<u>them and this is wrong. You cannot hide behind religions of men to justify your actions – wrongs. Earth was created free with true love and no government or human being on the face of this planet has or have a right to make another human being feel worthless or unwanted.</u> Good God did not make slaves nor did he make controlled beings – humans. You infinitely do not have a right to control your citizens nor do you have a right to tell them what to do in their own bedrooms. **Who a person chooses to truly love is his or her God given right. It is no one's right to tell a person who to truly love. This is between them and Good God. If Good God say that person is not right for you then he or she is not right for you – us. Good God sees what we as humans cannot see. This was evident in the case of Eve (Evening). She did not listen hence she fell from grace.**

KNOW THIS.

<u>GOOD GOD GIVETH NO MAN OR WOMAN THE RIGHT TO SPEAK ON HIS BEHALF IN THE SPIRITUAL AND ON HER BEHALF IN THE PHYSICAL IF HE HAS NOT CHOSEN YOU.</u>

87

If you are not a messenger of God – Good God then you do not have any right to speak on the behalf of Good God because he did not choose you.

HENCE NO MEMBER OF THE CLERGY CAN SAY THEY SPEAK FOR OR ON THE BEHALF OF GOOD GOD BECAUSE THEY KNOW NOT THE GOODNESS AND TRUTH OF GOD – GOOD GOD. THEY KNOW NOT GOD HENCE THEY SELL HUMANITY SIN AND DEATH.

GOOD GOD IS CLEAN NOT DIRTY. HENCE NO MEMBER OF THE CLERGY IS CLEAN THEY ARE DIRTY – FILTHY.

Preachers – the church community are thieves that rob Good God of his truth – his true people. But truly woe be unto them when death comes because they will pay and pay dearly when death is through with them. They, the clergy sell death and *Good God is not death he is true life.* Hence life begins with water and ends with water for the wicked. True life hath no end hence water – life will never end. This is why we are told ***TRUTH IS EVERLASTING LIFE. WITHOUT TRUTH NO ONE CAN HAVE EVERLASTING LIFE WITH GOOD GOD. ABSOLUTELY NO ONE. Come on now.***

IF THESE SO – CALLED RELIGIOUS LEADERS WERE SO CORRECT AND HOLY THEY WOULD KNOW THAT GOOD GOD IS MALE IN THE SPIRITUAL AND FEMALE IN THE PHYSICAL. LIKE I'VE SAID AND WILL FOR EVERY TELL HUMANITY, A DIRTY MAN OR WOMAN KNOWETH NOT GOD – GOOD GOD HENCE THEY CANNOT SPEAK FOR HIM. IF THEY – THESE PEOPLE WERE SO RIGHTEOUS AND HOLY NO ONE WOULD DIE BECAUSE WE WOULD ALL BE LIVING CLEAN – RIGHTEOUS.

IF YOUR CLERGY WAS SO RIGHTEOUS AND HOLY, RUSSIA WOULDN'T BE SLATED TO LOSE IT ALL AND HUMANITY WOULD NOT BE SLATED TO DIE BEFORE 2032. Your people are your people and as a government – any government that say they govern their people, you must treat each citizens fair and just. ***AS A GOVERNMENT YOU SAY YOU ARE RESPONSIBLE FOR YOUR PEOPLE BUT YET YOU TREAT YOUR PEOPLE LIKE SHIT.*** So tell me as government and governments globally what makes any of you right? ***YOU'RE ALL***

89

UNJUST AND IT IS BECAUSE OF YOUR UNJUST AND WARRING NATURE – SENSELESS MURDERS THE HARVEST COMES. *You too are to blame for this harvest along with humanity because if we did not kill and sin – do all manner of evil the harvest would not come.*

HENCE LIKE I SAID, WE (HUMAN BEINGS) ARE SINS SACRIFICE UNTO DEATH AND WE DON'T KNOW IT. We were told the wages of sin is death but instead of leaving sin alone we follow sin unto our deaths.

Shortly, Russia will lose it all and what say you? Good God does not dick around with the life of humans – his people. So why are you taking the rights of your people away? ***You too will be held guilty in Good God's court of Justice and by me seeing Russia casting its hose into the earth – well or hole and getting nothing in return tells me that your land have and has been judged in the court of Good God and found guilty as charged.*** Yes I've said God judges no one and it remains so but I do not have a better way to put things. What I need to say is because of the your sins and the sins that happens in your land on a daily basis you've been found guilty of lies, treason and injustice and your sentence is emptiness. Meaning your land must become

90

barren – void of life and food including water and resources.

Every individual have and has a right to live free and good and instead of providing for your people, you leave your children and adults starving – wanting. The billions that Russia spends on war each year is not right. For this, each land that funds Aries – the God of War have and has been found guilty. ***You are an adult. Not everyone is heterosexual. Homosexuals have been around since the beginning of time and before time. By banning or outlawing gays and lesbians you are banning Good God. You are telling Good God she is not wanted in your land hence she must leave.***

When she is gone your land will be left barren – without food and water – resources. So infinitely truly know what you are doing because you are infinitely wrong to ban Good God and his people.

Banning gay people is an injustice in the eyes and sight of Good God and no human being on the face of this planet can justify this wrong. Look at the human gene and tell me otherwise. Come on now. You are wrong in what you are doing hence Good God is against Russia ***because***

91

Russia sides with the HOUSES OF DEATH AND DEATH AGAINST HIM GOOD GOD.

HOMOSEXUALS ARE NOT THE UNJUST ONES. HETEROSEXUALS ARE THE UNJUST ONES.

And don't even think of coming after me with your **_RUSSIAN INEPT CLERGY_** because they've sinned massive. Worse than sin himself when it comes to the lies they tell – preach about Good God on a daily basis. *They preach and teach death hence they are all death's children. Wolves in sheep clothing. Vultures that scavenge on the flesh of humans.*

Oh trust me I will elaborate further on in this book so continue to read. Trust me I will let loose but for now I cannot let my spirit take control of me. I have to press on in a good way not a wrathful way.

And no government dare say you have to protect your land from invaders. Like I said, **_immigration is a weapon because instead of feeding our own we take others from other lands that care nothing for your land and drain your economy – system._** *We are the ones to keep our people and children starving while we feed the children of the Babylonians.*

92

Keep the Babylonians in their own damned country. They are a pollution hence none is found on the mountain with Good God and his children. ***WHY THE HELL SHOULD YOU TAKE THE FOOD OFF THE TABLE OF YOUR CHILDREN AND PEOPLE – LAND AND FEED THEM (THE BABYLONIANS).*** I know some of you are saying it's the godly thing to do. But let me ask you this, *when did Good God give you the Babylonians?*

When did Good God tell you that the Babylonians were his people? But but you said Good God – God does not lock anyone out of his kingdom. Infinitely true, hence I also said, WE ARE THE ONES TO LOCK OURSELVES OUT OF HIS KINGDOM – GOOD GOD'S KINGDOM - ABODE.
DID THEY (THE BABYLONIANS) NOT LIE TO YOU TO GET INTO YOUR KINGDOM AND BRING YOU TO HELL WITH THEM?

DO THEY NOT TELL LIES ON GOOD GOD AND HIS CHILDREN?

DID THEY NOT LIE TO EVE AND CAUSE HER TO DIE AND DISGRACE GOOD GOD?

DO THEY NOT LIE TO YOU AND HAVE YOU BELIEVING IN A FALSE GOD TO BRING YOUR SOUL AND SPIRIT TO HELL WITH THEM?

93

DO THEY NOT HAVE YOU DRINKING BLOOD AND COMMITTING HUMAN SACRIFICES UNTO THEIR FILTHY GODS SO THAT YOU CAN GO TO HELL AND DIE WITH THEM?

DO THEY NOT HATE GOOD GOD TO THE POINT WHERE IF THEY CANNOT GET INTO GOOD GOD'S ABODE THEY ARE GOING TO DESTROY GOD'S CREATION AND TAKE HUMANITY WITH THEM?

IS THIS NOT WHAT THEY ARE DOING TODAY?

IS THIS NOT WHAT YOU AS AN INDIVIDUAL IS DOING TODAY?

ARE YOU NOT DESTROYING SELF AND GOOD GOD TO GO TO HELL AND BURN WITH WICKED AND EVIL PEOPLE. SINFUL BEINGS – HUMAN BEINGS THAT ARE NOT OF GOOD GOD?

Like I said, you can save yourself but you have to want it. ***Hell is not pretty so why want to go there and die senselessly?*** Look at it this way also. When you go to hell, your children are going there with you because you would have taught your children wrong also. So the lies you were taught you teach your children, hence they live in lies along with you and they die alongside you.

94

All they (The Babylonians) do is lie to you and keep you sinning. Know the truth of them because **_GOOD GOD DID TRY TO PROTECT YOU FROM THEM HENCE THE LAND OF GAD – GOOD GOD AND NOD._** Good God has and have been trying to protect us from them but we keep going into the fire. Hell is their home so why go there with them? *They are the ones to have the many gods and idols. We know this but yet instead of keeping your CLEAN AND GOOD UP, GOOD UP GOD, WE TAKE ON THEIR FILTHY AND NASTY STINKING GODS AND BECOME STINK LIKE THEM, HENCE WE CANNOT KEEP OUR BODIES CLEAN WE PASS FILTH JUST LIKE THEM.*

In a way I am glad God – Good God did not choose me to go into politics because immigration would be banned when it comes to certain countries. The devil's own could not come into my land. I would cry tears greater than rivers and seas when it comes to me petitioning God not to let wicked and evil people including the devil's own into our land. Who the hell wants sin's people to come into their land and pollute it? I would be like GOOOOOOOOOOOOOOOOOOD they are trying to come into our land. Gooooooooooooooooooooood get rid of them. Gooooooooooooooooooooood put a river that is clear and hotter than infinite suns that can burn the spirit harsh and brutal

95

around our land so that they cannot come in. Gooooooooooooooood activate your invisible force field that is as hot like our clear river so that when they try to drop in unannounced they cannot come in – they disintegrate. Gooooooooooooooood let earth take away all their resources so that they cannot build bombs, chemicals, diseases of any sort or form to harm us. Gooooooooooooooooood let there be no escape for them from hell because they did choose hell as their home so let them stay in hell and burn. And Good God, I so don't want to hear them or see their burning faces – carcass before me. Trust me God – Good God would keep them out especially if the land and people is living right good and true by him. Infinitely trust me that land would be well protected from all evil because **_RETURN TO SENDER WOULD SURROUND THE LAND AND PEOPLE._** Whatever evil tries would go right back to evil. Bombs that they try to let off would detonate in their own land. Nothing evil do will or would prosper hence **_NO WEAPONS FORMED AGAINST GOD – GOOD GOD AND HIS PEOPLE WILL OR SHALL PROSPER. INFINITELY NO WAY. THIS I KNOW BECAUSE GOD – GOOD GOD IS THE TRUE KEEPER OF HIS PEOPLE – CHILDREN._** No land of Good God or people of Good God would be in debt because when we least expect it we get. **_This I can state and_**

96

skate my reputation on when it comes to Good God hence I truly love him so.

So to Russia, you are warned and you know what will befall you if you do not clean up your act. One had a solid ripe mango in her hand yes. Hence I tell you all is not lost for your country but it's up to you to accept Good God and his truth. Look at the world and see the mess. Clean your land up and respect your people. ***Feed them and cut down on your defense spending as well because in this harvest war will become a thing of the past. Food and Water will become essential. Food and Water will be the cry of each and every land that is not under the banner of Good God.*** You can be like America and reject the truth and warning of Good God and continue on the path of destruction, or you can ask God – Good God for forgiveness and turn your land around. Good God will show you what to do if you truly ask him in honesty and in truth.

Like I said, I do not care if the world hates me nor do I care if you Vladimir and Barack hates me. I do not care if either of you want to lynch my ass because at the end of the day ***I've delivered the message of God – Good God to both of you.*** Hence I know my tears and woe be unto man if they denounce me and Good God meaning the words of Good God. I will not

97

hesitate to tell Good God to leave – go because you rejected him. I've done it before hence many countries have been judged and sentenced. *See The New Book of Life – Judgement.* And humanity don't think this warning goes for Russia alone. It goes for every child and country of Good God on and in this planet. Every child must prepare for the harvest because like I said, **_CANNIBALISM WILL BE A REALITY_** because we made it so. **_Do not be like the people of Noah's days, be like the people of Daniel and prepare yourself._** Gather up – store up your good blessings for the severe drought that is to come.

I did see BLACK and WHITE death together and they had – one had the scroll of death in his hand so make sure your name is not written in death's book because if it is, good luck when death comes around because you would be too late. If you go to the house of death and pay for death, good luck to you when death comes because you will not survive this harvest you will be too late also. **_RESPECT GOD – GOOD GOD AND LIVE CLEAN._** *Good God never gave us whore houses and the houses of the deceitful and thieves to worship him in.* THE WRITING ON THE WALL SAID, **_"FOR GOD SO LOVE US HE IS WORTHY TO BE PRAISED."_** It means we are to thank him for the goodness he's blessed us with.

We can no longer be ungrateful.

We can no longer live for death.

We can no longer live for sin.

We must live for life – good life.

God – Good God asked me to write a book and I've written many like I've said in my other books. *I do not require or need your soul or spirit because you need it. Good God gave it to you good and you are to take care of it. Your soul or spirit is yours and it is not right for someone to come along and rob you of it. Your spirit is that energy inside of you and you are to keep it clean and pure. So as humans we have to truly think.* If you are not sure of me **_TRULY GO TO GOD – GOOD GOD AND TELL HIM THAT YOU ARE NOT SURE OF ME._** Do not take these words at face value. You can talk to God but go to him in truth – clean. **_No one can stop you from speaking to Good God but you._** No one can intercede for you. Good God never said that person is the one that must speak for you. **_IF YOU ARE LIVING IN TRUTH THEN YOU ARE GOOD TO GO BECAUSE TRUTH IS EVERLASTING LIFE AND NO ONE CAN CHANGE THIS._** God gave you a mouth – a silent voice, use it to connect with God – Good God. And no Good God does not like ruckus – noise. God is silent hence your silent spirit – words.

And infinitely yes, yes, yes you can charge these whore houses known as Churches, Mosques, Synagogues, Shrines and Temple's TAXES. Good God does not need money nor does he use money so what do these churches need it for?

Can a man tax life?

Can a man tax Good God? So why are these people – filthy churches trying to tax him – rob him Good God of everything?

Say it when it comes to these books so I can tell you what to kiss. I do not sell death nor do I sell life hence soon I will no longer write these books. Life must come hence the New Book of Life - Life must be written. Then I will be done in the Michelle Jean series of books I think because I can say I am done and Good God say no honey you are not done.

Why the hell should the devil live free and the people of the land go broke and hungry?

Good God told no one he required 10% or 1/10th of their earnings.
Tell me something, can a man or anyone buy Good God?

Can anyone buy life?

No we cannot. But we sure as hell can buy death. Hence death is what you buy when you go to these churches hence death requires his pay because the **_wages_** of sin is death.

Bunch of thieves robbing Good God and man. So to the clergy stop using Good God to rob people. Stop mocking Good God because good life cannot defile anyone hence Good God cannot defile period.

Humans defile.

Enough is enough now man come on now. Good God does not rob you so why rob him?

Why use his name in your thieving schemes of death?

Fiya fi unnu literally. In the name of God and Good God fiya fi unnu. To hell all of you must go you demons of hell. In the name of God and Good God I condemn all of you to hell for infinite and indefinite lifetimes and generations to come. Allelujah FIYA – hell must come and claim his own. Thus saith/sayeth the Lord thy God meaning it is so.

Allelujah you are our true King – good life and no one must use you or your name for their evil agenda. Hence every preacher, pastor, deacon, bishop, priest and imam including those I have not mentioned are condemned. Their names as well as their families name, wife and children MUST BE TAKEN FROM YOUR GOOD BOOK OF LIFE INFINITELY AND INDEFINITELY. None must be found in any of your good records Good God hence DEATH NOW LITERALLY HAVE AND HAS THEM. Death must now update his record and add their names to his record. Thus saith/sayeth the Lord thy God meaning it is so. Absolutely none can change or override this decree Good God not even you. Death is death and death hath nothing to do with you Good God hence death children cannot be a part of your own.

We are humans are the ones to choose death.
We are the ones to accept his offering.
We made the choice not you Good God. It is man that must correct his or her wrongs. Come on now. We can't rely on you for everything. No scrap that because I rely on you for everything.

*You are not humanities garbage chute. You are Good God and it's time you truly walk away from man – humanity and let death take us. **Genesis showed us the lie did not work for Eve (Evening) and***

103

__instead of rejecting the lie meaning walk away from sin we continue to accept him and do for him.__ Good God we keep calling to you and say you are the one that we need but yet we cannot give up sin. Tell me something, how does that work? We can't sing glory unto you if we are dirty and stink. Come on now. You won't hear us hence you do not hear us today because we are unclean. Come on now.

We are the ones to prove to you time and time again that humanity – humans cannot be trusted. So why try to save us if you cannot trust us Good God? Yes I know why but I have to ask the question yet again.

Let me tell you this and know this, ***__anyone can hear the dead cry like a bitch in hell but because there is so much noise around us we cannot hear them.__*** Remember Natural Mystic by Bob Marley? Well over stand the song because he was trying to teach you something but you could not comprehend.

Man I've went beyond 32 pages so listen. It's up to every human being to listen to what Good God is trying to tell you and do good and well for self. Remember Noah did what Good God told him to do. He never strayed from the backlash of his people. He kept going even when the odds and people were against him and in the end he ***Noah did not fail Good God. Everyone around him failed hence they were not saved.*** Do not be like those people. LIKE I WILL SAID AND WILL FOREVER TELL YOU. ***I INFINITELY AND INDEFINITELY DO NOT WANT OR NEED YOUR SOULS OR SPIRIT.*** *MY SOUL AND SPIRIT IS SECURE WITH GOOD GOD ALREADY HENCE THE GOODNESS I DO MUST GO TO SAVING MY CHILDREN AND FAMILY, INCLUDING THE ONES GOOD GOD HAS AND HAVE ENTRUSTED ME WITH. MY GOODNESS MUST ALSO GO FOR MY MOM AND FAMILY INCLUDING GOOD GOD THAT ARE BEFORE ME – FURTHER IN TIME.* These family members are not dead because their spirit is still alive and well. Like I said, truth cannot die hence I do in goodness and truth all around – all the time.

I NEED YOU TO LIVE GOOD AND CLEAN FOR GOOD GOD SO THAT WHEN DEATH COMES AROUND TO TAKE THE SOULS OR SPIRITS OF MAN – HUMANITY, HE DEATH PASSES OVER YOU AND YOUR FAMILY. BUT IF YOU AND YOUR FAMILY ARE NOT LIVING CLEAN AND GOOD

105

DEATH CANNOT PASS OVER YOU HE OR SHE MUST TAKE YOU.

Like I've said, male death is not as fierce or deadly because when you can stop ***MALE DEATH IN THE LIVING YOU CANNOT STOP FEMALE DEATH TO A CERTAIN DEGREE.***

As messengers you do not want to piss off female death because she is worse than a bulldozer. She takes everything hence female death is to be feared. She is the end all to everything. Hence it is a female that receives sin's children at the gate (s) of hell. You now know this hence do good and don't try to go to hell. ***If you cheat slowly cut it out because the respect and true love of Good God is everything.***

OH MY FAMILY AND PEOPLE, GOOD REGGAE IS BACK. PEOPLE AND FAMILY PLEASE BUY THIS SONG ON ITUNES FOR ME. IT'S CALLED FIGHT THIS FEELING BY BERES HAMMOND AND SHAGGY.

Family, I am truly in love again. Wow. Tune brap brap brap. Big up and pull up.
George, if you did not hate my ass after what I wrote in this book and others I would truly dance to this song with you for real. No for real people.

106

This song I truly want to dance with someone to. I know Tyrese but he's faded in my book for some strange reason. Sorry Tyrese my belly is no longer available. It's off limits now. Shaq you're still in my book. So can't get rid of you. Maybe it's because you are a giant in my book and you are my fun and play book wise. So Shaq when Jamaica is cleaned up, if it gets cleaned up, think of the children in my homeland and spend some time there. Even if it's 2 weeks teaching inner city youths basketball. And Shaq all cost must be on you because the kids are poor. I'm batting my eyes and pouting like a child if you protest. Hopefully the batting of the eyes and pouting works hence pleeeease.

As for you expats that have children. Send unnu pickney dem back a yaade fi help. Nuff a unnu pickney dem have one parent, nuff ha two parents that are of Jamaican decent hence dem ha Jamaican. Help unnu country because nuff a unnu pickney dem ha money but yet dem naah help Jamaica. Unnu bane lan a Jamaica but unnu no teach unnu pickney dem fi help unnu bane lan. Unnu a Jamaican – children that was born unto Good God but yet unnu tun from yaade. Help di country. Unnu pickney dem have an obligation to Good God – Jamaica because Good God did make us hence we are the true Judahites – the TRUE JEWS. Wake up now man. ***JAMAICA IS GOING TO BE***

107

DESTROYED and we are the cause of it. If we can turn Jamaica around and save the land we must. We have to save Jamaica because we are blessed but we turned that blessing into a curse.

HONESTLY RIGHT NOW. AUGUST 19, 2013 I AM GRIEVING – WANT TO CRY. I am editing this book and I am truly hurting because I want and need to go back home but cannot. Every time I tell Good God I want to go home ***I smell smoke – breadfruit burning.*** Trust me, I keep bugging Good God and last week – week of August 17, 2013 I was told ***JAMAICA IS NOT CLEAN – IT'S DIRTY. SO IF I GO ON OR INTO THE LAND I WILL BECOME UNCLEAN – DIRTY LIKE THE LAND AND PEOPLE.***

Do you know how hurtful it is to hear Jamaica is unclean?

Do you know how hurtful it is to hear Good God tell you that your homeland (Jamaica) is unclean – dirty?

Do you know how shameful this is?
Good God told me people – humanity that the land he gave to me at birth is

unclean? JAMAICA IS MY RIGHT. NOW I NO LONGER HAVE THAT RIGHT BECAUSE MY OWN PEOPLE TOOK THAT FROM ME AND GOOD GOD.

JAMAICA IS GOOD GOD'S RIGHT. AND HE CAN NO LONGER ENJOY THAT RIGHT BECAUSE MY OWN PEOPLE LITERALLY TOOK HIS RIGHT FROM HIM AND MADE HIS NAME AND LAND INCLUDING THE BREATH OF LIFE UNCLEAN – DIRTY.

NOW TELL ME WHAT DOES JAMAICA HAVE LEFT?

GOOD GOD DEEMED LAND AND PEOPLE UNCLEAN – DIRTY. THIS IS DIRECTLY COMING FROM GOOD GOD.

We had ALLELUJAH and we literally gave it away – sold it. No one on the face of the planet had Allelujah apart from us. No one could lay claim to Allelujah but Jamaica and Jamaicans could and we sold it for a piece of Satan's mouldy and stinky bread of filth.

We bleeping had ALL you dumb asses.

109

We literally had Good God not just in spirit but in name and land and we literally gave him up to feast with Satan at his table of stench.

BLEEP!! DO YOU TRULY KNOW WHAT YOU HAVE DONE?

Do you? No wonder we have no value when it comes to ambition and pride – truth.

BECAUSE NOT EVEN GOOD GOD CAN TRUST US.

From Eve (Evening) cum slap back to wi now a day's people.

We've proven death – Satan right when it comes to trust.

Death did tell Good God he was going to make him feel it – prove him wrong

110

when it came to his people and so said so done.

We made Satan right and no one on the face of this planet can dispute this.

No one in the black race can prove me wrong because all I have to do is point to our disgrace history from Evening (Eve) of the book of sin to all the lands of Africa including the Caribbean.

Do you know the hurt and pain I feel to know that my disgusting.....no let me stop because hell will have no fury like mine if I go off.

I truly have to calm myself because you know what the bleeping Black Race is not worth it. Hence HELL IS FULL OF BLACK PEOPLE AND RECRUITING MORE LIKE I'VE SAID.

Yes it's a bleeping disgrace and sad state – day to hear Good God himself say Jamaica is unclean. But this is the reality of the black race – people today. Untrustworthy hence we treat our own people in the manner that we do.

We rob our country of its wealth
We rob our children of their good future
We treat our own like crap – shit literally
We rape our women and women literally
We turn our children into fools that lack worth, education – value. Hence we've become valueless in the sight of Good God and man - humanity.

We've become a liability to Good God hence the trust is gone literally. But then again we were never his asset but the devil's weapon against him Good God. And yes you can take it as you see it because I will never make any apologies to any of you for this statement.

We turn our countries into killing fields – the killing fields of death hence all that Good God has and have given us has and have become unclean – dirty.

YES YOU THE BLACK RACE CAN DISPUTE ME. BUT TO DISPUTE ME IS TO SAY TO GOOD GOD IN HIS FACE HE IS LYING – HE'S A LIAR. If you doubt me go directly to Good God and ask him if he told me this. He will tell you yes. Good God cannot tell you otherwise because I've been bugging him to go back home and now I can't thanks to my own deg....(never mind) people.

113

Do you know how hurtful it is to know that Good God gave us his name, the breath of life, his goodness and good being and we polluted him – the land and his spirit all around? Hence I cuss us – Jamaicans so. We destroyed Good God. We trampled Good God down. This morning August 19, 2013 I dreamt the upward triangle with eye at the foot or feet of man and I was upset at Good God. We trample life down because life is at our sole – feet. Yes I see many things but ***HOW THE HELL CAN HUMANITY GIVE UP LIFE FOR DEATH?*** Yes I am mad but this is not the book for it. Yes another book is to come and humanity will more than hate me when I am through.

Jamaicans we made Jamaica the killing field of wickedness.
We made Jamaica the land for vile and disgusting monsters that rape and kill little children at will.

We talk but yet we care not.

Port Royal sank in June 1692, Hurricane Gilbert, Ivan, Sandy+ have ravished the land and still we continue to do wickedness and cry to Good God for help.

People obeah people without remorse and still unnu continue to sin.

11⁴

WHAT DOES IT TAKE JAMAICA?

If you change not then your doom will be your own. You cannot sin daily and expect Good God to be pleased with you.

Look how many people suffering right now.

Look at your child that's hungry and tell them why they have to suffer like that? *And don't you dare lie to them and tell them no slavery bullshit because we the black race sold our own to death long ago.*

Tell them the truth of Jamaica's sins – Jamaicans.

Tell the truth of how the Judas Labour Party (JLP) sold out the land including Air God – the Breath of Life and Doctor Bird – the healing of the nation in air.

Tell them.

Tell them how the People's National Pimps (PNP) sold the people for little a nothing.

Tell them about the evils that Jamaicans do on a daily basis without remorse.

115

Tell them you're all loyal to death, hence you sold your own including Good God and land to become a part of the devil's deceitful own.

Like I said evil breeds evil. So how can a nation of vipers bring forth anything good? Say it. Go ahead and say it so I can truly tell all of you, bleep you.

Truss mi I truly don't know because all the destruction you've had, have not caused you to change your vile ways. Maybe now when brimstone and fire level unnu and bun unnu, unnu wi learn. But I doubt that. The only way unnu wi learn is when Jamaica wipe off the map and then it will be too late for all of you. You'll all be in hell burning harsher than a bitch in heat.

SO ANYONE THAT GOES TO JAMAICA NOW – AS OF AUGUST 19, 2013 WILL BECOME UNCLEAN – DIRTY IN THE EYES AND SIGHT OF GOOD GOD.

ANYONE THAT MARRIES ON THE LAND THEIR MARRIAGE WILL BECOME UNCLEAN – DIRTY IN THE EYES AND SIGHT OF GOOD GOD.

ANYONE THAT NOW DIES ON THE LAND AND IS BURIED ON OR IN THE LAND WILL BECOME UNCLEAN – DIRTY IN THE EYES AND SIGHT OF GOOD GOD.

Note: Spiritual time is not the same as Physical time. I say August 19, 2013 because this is the

day I had the dream so count 3-9 months from now. 9 months being the extreme or longest time frame given. NO THIS IS NOT RIGHT, HENCE THE PHYSICAL AND SPIRITUAL TIME EXPLANATION DOES NOT FLY. I WILL BE GIVING YOU FALSE HOPE AND INFORMATION AND I TRULY CANNOT DO THIS. I'VE BEEN BUGGING GOOD GOD ABOUT THIS (GOING TO MY HOMELAND FOR A VACATION) FOR A LONG TIME AND HE DID ANSWER ME, SO I CANNOT SAY 3-9 MONTHS AFTER. AS OF AUGUST 19, 2013 JAMAICA HAS AND HAVE BECOME UNCLEAN – DIRTY BECAUSE IT IS ON THIS DAY THAT GOOD GOD TOLD ME MICHELLE JAMAICA IS UNCLEAN - DIRTY. SO ANYONE THAT GO TO JAMAICA OR MARRY ON OR IN THE LAND OF JAMAICA AS OF AUGSUT 19, 2013 WILL BE UNCLEAN – DIRTY.

Yes repentance is there for those that have scheduled their wedding in advance. You can ask Good God not to make your wedding unclean – dirty because of prior booking. Good God does comprehend – overstand and understand.

Further, because Jamaica has and have become unclean – dirty in the eyes and sight of Good God, no one can allow any Jamaican from Jamaica entrance to enter into your land (s). Any country that does this will become dirty –

unclean in the eyes and sight of Good God also. If you disobey, whatever the punishment that is set out for Jamaica and Jamaican will befall your land worse than the punishment they get. You would have disobeyed Good God and his direct law – order.

THE ONLY TIME YOU CAN ALLOW ANY JAMAICAN FROM JAMAICA ACCESS TO YOUR LAND IS IF THEY TRULY REPENT AND BECOME CLEAN.

Some of you may be saying whatever I don't believe in God or Good God anyway.

Hey you were warned.

You can go into the land because unclean would be going to unclean BUT THE CHILDREN OF GOOD GOD CANNOT ENTER THE LAND. THIS IS A SPECIFIC ORDER. THE ONLY TIME WE CAN GO BACK HOME IS IF THE LAND AND PEOPLE REPENT AND BECOME CLEAN. ONCE THEY ARE CLEAN GOOD GOD'S PEOPLE CAN GO BACK THERE AND ENJOY HIM. THIS I YEARN FOR. I AM TRULY HOPING THAT JAMAICANS WILL TURN AROUND AND TAKE THEIR DIRTY SHEETS OFF THEIR BEDS AND GET RID OF THE COAT OF ARMS THEY HAVE IN THE JAMAICAN HOUSE OF PARLIAMENT. WE DO NOT NEED THE DEVIL'S COAT OF ARMS. WE NEED THE LIFE AND GOODNESS OF GOOD GOD INFINITELY AND INDEFINITELY.

In as much, if you go to the land of Jamaica for business, pleasure or otherwise you will become

118

BLACKMAN REDEMPTION – THE DEATH OF RUSSIA

*dirty – unclean. **There will be no forgiveness for this because you now know and you were warned. I know many of us will travel for death – death in the family but if you are a child of Good God you cannot go into the land of Jamaica because the land is not clean. You will become dirty and filthy like them and Good God will turn from you – not know you.** So truly know what you are doing because you are being warned. **YOU WERE TOLD HENCE NONE OF YOU CAN SAY GOOD GOD, I DID NOT KNOW. IF YOU DO THEN YOU WOULD BE LYING BECAUSE YOU WERE TOLD IN THIS BOOK – ABOVE. And yes Good God can and will charge you for willful sin – lies.***

So Russia truly think. My homeland is unclean do not make yours unclean. Like I said, you have a saving grace so use it well. Maybe the desolation I see is going to come in the form of a bomb. So be on your guard especially in the winter games. But by me saying this – using a bomb is me grappling at straws. I did not see fire nor did I see destruction associated with water. Your land is going to be desolate so figure out the dream because I truly can't. When it happens then the oh that's what the dream meant will hit. Dry dreams are not my favorite. I cannot pinpoint them nor do I know how to decipher them hence I tell you to figure it out for yourselves. Your so-called clergies say they are of God – Good God so let them do their work. In regards to your economy I cannot say this dream is associated with it because I did not see the downfall of your economy. The only person I've seen losing his wealth so far is Prokhorov. He too must know what he's doing because he is being warned. This is not the time for greed or amassing more fortune. This is the time to store up food and water and if you're wealthy you must protect your wealth but good luck with that. ***FOOD AND WATER IS GOING TO BECOME SCARCE. AND IT IS THE MAN OR COUNTRY WITH THE FOOD AND WATER THAT WILL BECOME THE WEALTHIEST MAN OR LAND ON THE FACE OF THE PLANET.***

Your idols and gods that you believe in must provide for his people because it is false idols and gods' humanity believe in. So truly good luck to the lots of you. Truly, truly good luck because I know for a fact that none of your false gods and idols can or will help you. Fact is, they can't period. ***Good God must take his blessings from man – humanity because humanity did not choose him.*** Go back to Noah of your book of sin. Noah preached to the people by telling them to prepare for rain and they laughed at him. *Their gods were not Noah's god hence Noah's god saved him and death took his own.* ***TODAY IS NO DIFFERENT BECAUSE***

120

THIS IS THE TIME OF NOAH, DANIEL, MOSES, JOHN THE BAPTIST, JONAH, RUTH+ ROLLED UP INTO ONE. It's either you are on board with Good God now or you will be left behind. There are no ands ifs or buts about this. ***THIS IS REALITY.*** You can all point fingers, accuse me, laugh at me. That's fine. It matters not to me because I know my tears and anger. Trust me I'm already in Good God's Ark.

If you choose to wait until that final hour – second, good luck because you will never get in. This I know for a fact. Hence it is guaranteed.

JUST A LITTLE FOOTNOTE BEFORE I MOVE ON.

LIKE I SAID, YOU THE WHITE RACE ARE THE SICK RACE OR THE SIKH RACE NOT THE NODITES – BABYLONIANS. KNOW THIS TO BE TRUE SO RECLAIM YOUR HISTORY AND HERITAGE.

This has nothing to do with wrapping your head, it has to do with truth and true love when it comes to Good God. ***It also has to do with sickness and once I get the full truth I will so infinitely let you know.*** Just keep true truth in mind because despite what the black race say you are truly blessed and highly favoured by Good God. So down with the racism okay because Good God favours you. And please hold your head up because this has nothing to do with colour of skin. ***WHITE PEOPLE ARE IN GOOD GOD'S ABODE CONTRARY TO WHAT SOME BLACK PEOPLE SAY. YOU ARE NOT CURSED LIKE THE MUSLIMS WOULD HAVE US BELIEVE. AND IF I'VE SAID YOU ARE THE CURSED RACE IN ANY OF MY OTHER BOOKS, I DO ASK FOR FORGIVENESS IN TRUTH AND TRUE LOVE.***

ONWARDS I GO NOW

Shaggy, Laade mi nah go dey because wi affi stan up and dweet. Easy wifey a dance and book talk. Beres hopefully one day I get to meet you. I truly thank you for continuing the vibe when it comes to good and clean reggae music. Your sex talk is clean and I truly like that. Never stop giving us good reggae music because we do need it. ***Reggae back people hence Beres I have to give you a nice candle light dinner if Good God permits it.***

Tune my youth, good clean tune. Shaggy you are back yes. Truly thank you for bringing back clean music. So any day you want mi fi bi yu empress truss mi I am more than willing and able. Never mind as I am into book talk and true respect must be given to your wife – empress. ***Sly and Robbie I need my hour of studio time with the both of you. The both of you can and will teach me a thing or two when it comes to making rhythm and mixing down the rhythm.***

Wow.

Family trust me, I can make a tune for God – Good God when it comes to this song. Trust me, if this song was sung another way I would dedicate it to God – Good God.

So God, because I truly love and respect you. If I could give you everything you desire I would give it to you and more. No one could or would come between us because I do go out of control and over board when it comes to you.

Good God wi boasy but unfortunately I am not proper. You are the proper one God – Good God because fi mi mouth no ha no kinna. Mi a cussa and when mi cuss down to death haffi shut up.

So God because I truly love you like that. I need you to love me more than more.
Yes people I am going crazy off and on this song hence the few lines above. Trust mi people if God

coulda hold me tight wow. People not even the universes could contain my glee – happiness. You know wha mi betta stop because I am salivating just thinking about God – Good God. Yes people God is that wow in my eyes.

So truly love Good God because he does truly love us. I will tell you again, **_THE LIFE YOU LIVE IN THE LIVING DETERMINES WHERE YOU GO IN THE GRAVE – AFTER LIFE._**

I WILL ALSO TELL YOU YET AGAIN. GOD – GOOD GOD DID NOT LOCK US OUT OF HIS ABODE. WE AS HUMANS LOCKED OURSELVES OUT OF HIS ABODE WITH THE LIES WE TELL AND THE SINS WE DO ON A DAILY BASIS.

LIES ARE SINS AND IT IS UP TO US TO BECOME TRUTHFUL IN ALL THAT WE DO.

We can no longer have good life at our feet and expect Good God to clean up or mess. Like I said, we make the mess and we are the ones to clean it up. Life is not death but good life. We are to take care of good life and live clean because no dirty preacher, person, lawyer, murderer, adulterer or any sinful thing of the sort can live to see Good God. **_They must die to see death hence when a politician kill – go_**

to war to fight another man's war he the politician put his country and people in debt. They make your land sin against Good God hence the sins your political leaders do affect you as a people – nation. There are no ands ifs or buts about this because it is reality. It is so and no politician can dispute this because it is written – recorded. All that you do to country and people are recorded on your slate – record and woe be unto you when death is done sentencing you. Every soldier you send to war to kill, (his name) is recorded on your slate – record. You are responsible for their deaths hence you are all like unto David the murderer in the book of sin. None of you can or will save self because you've all committed willful and sinful murders in the eyes and sight of God – Good God. Hence many, if not all of you are locked out of Good God's kingdom just like the Babylonians. And you'll can thank the Babylonians for this because many of you murder for them for oil – money – profit including prophets. And none of you can dispute this. The facts, records and murders are there for humanity to see – watch on television, the internet and so forth. Hence your sins are witnessed and recorded before Good God and Man – humanity.

And people do not give away your possessions when it comes to this

125

harvest. **_Store up for it (the harvest)_** **_meaning be stingy with water and food._** *If Good God – God tells me which land his people are to move to I will let you know.* **_Wicked and evil people need not apply or come because God – Good God will let none of you in. You are the ones death is coming to take and he must take all of you because in all you do, you did not remember Good God – God._**

People remember to buy Fight This Feeling by Shaggy and Beres Hammond.

In all that I do, thank you and may Good God truly touch your lives with goodness – his good blessings. Stay strong and firm to God – Good God because truth is worth it.

Good God is the truth. He is also life so truly love him and life.

Like I said, no one can tell you how to truly love him (Good God) because your relationship with him is your own. So slowly move away from evil and wickedness. I say slowly because no one can give up all they use to do just like that. It takes time and patience so take baby steps. It will not be easy but **_TRUE AND GOOD LIFE IS WORTH IT._**

When you are true and honest with Good God your life becomes easier. I'm a single parent and trust me I nag God – Good God about it. I truly love raising my children despite the hardships I faced and still face with them. Yes I want to give them away sometimes but that's when the stresses of life gets to me that's all. No I have to say I truly love raising them because God has helped me to raise my children. Yes it was hard but the hardness is leaving. God is providing for me so now I cannot complain anymore. ***I am almost debt free and I truly love it.*** Once these three debts are paid off I can lift my hand to glory and say Good God we made it. We made it, truly thank you.

People despite the storm Good God is with us but you have to cling to him and stay true to him.

We cuss our kids; say why did I give birth to you? I wish I never had children but there are no undo buttons when it comes to humanity and sending our children up the birth canal and get another one.

There are no send him or her button back to get a child to your specifications – specific needs once they are born. Hence I drill it into the heads of those who have not children as well as those who want more children to give Good God your need list before you have children and or have more. Ask Good God for good, clean, obedient, progressive, smart and truthful children that will cling to his good family values as well as him.

ONWARDS I GO

Trust me no one can come to my door and sell me their false and dirty deities – gods. As soon as they come I tell them I am fine. Okay. I do not need their god or gods people. Some tell me God loves everyone and I have to tell them NO. GOD DOES NOT LOVE EVERYONE. GOOD GOD IS TRUTH PEOPLE ***HOW CAN HE TRULY LOVE WICKED AND EVIL PEOPLE? PEOPLE WHO KNOWINGLY HURT OTHERS – YOU.*** *Let no one, absolutely no one tell you that God loves everyone. GOD – GOOD GOD DOES NOT LOVE HE TRULY LOVES. HE TRULY LOVES US SO hence he's put up with our disobedience for so long but no more.*

No child of God can love or truly love evil and injustice. We cannot hence to the Martin family – Trayvon Martin's family, if you are true to God let God bring justice and closure to your family. Because injustice was done unto you and your family. I am telling you to take your cries to Good God not Jesus and let God – Good God bring you justice. This man killed your son

128

wrongfully so let Good God handle him and the people that made him walk free. Never pray evil for this man because Good God is the vindicator for his true people. When man – humanity showeth not justice, Good God gives you justice and victory. That victory is knowing that your enemies are going to go to hell and burn. ***Trust me, no one will save them in the grave. So truly hold on to Good God and smile because you have victory over him already. You also have victory over every juror, judge, his family and children know that. If only you knew hence hold on, hold on, truly hold on and dry your tears. Smile because none will see Good God this I know. Michelle Jean.***

Flesh we cannot bring back – no one can. Know that the flesh is a conductor for the spirit. We can see our loved ones but because our eyes are not clear enough we cannot see them in their resting state. Wicked people we see because there is no resting place for them hence they walk the earth and plague humanity but not for long. Hence 40 days of roaming the earth but it's not forty days it's longer. Worry not about evil spirit because their time has come. They too must face this harvest and woe be unto them.

We all need God – Good God but many have chosen Death over Life. Right now it is death for death when it comes to man hence they have no place with Good God. They have a place with death hence death will and must take them.

This harvest is going to be brutal hence billions will not survive it because they made it so. Like I said, worry not yourself because Good God is truly on your side. Know this and live up not down because your son has been vindicated. Hold on to your victory because shortly everyone that sided with this man will pay – must pay because they did wrong. The judge, the jurors, the people that helped this man, the police that aided him, including those that enacted the Stand Your Ground Law will pay and pay dearly. The harvest is not for good people but for every evil and wicked person that has and have sinned against Good God and his people from day one. Like I said, the church – preachers of the church are liars – evil and of evil. No one will save the wicked in the grave. Absolutely no one (PSALMS ONE). When they tell you someone died for your sins, they are infinitely and indefinitely going against **THE LAW AND LAWS OF GOOD GOD** because the law of sin states, **"THE WAGES OF SIN IS DEATH."** So when they go against this law and tell you otherwise (a man died for your sins) they are going against Good God and the direct law of sin. The wages of sin is death is sin's law not Good God because good cannot sin nor can good die.

Sin requires your life hence he has humanity – humans sinning and that's why he enacted his law. HENCE THE WAGES OF SIN IS DEATH.

BUT TRUTH IS EVERLASTING LIFE – ETERNAL LIFE.

Like I said, no one can die for your sins. You are accountable for them. The plain truth is. *If you do not live good and clean there is no way that you are going to live to see Good God.* Your sins are recorded on your slate or in your record book and *no one can give account for them except for you.* The next person or man does not know what is in your record – slate so how the hell can he give an account for your sins? You sinned, hence you know your sin and sins not the next man or person. So when you say Jesus died for your sins, good look with that because no one can die to make you see *LIFE – GOOD GOD. ABSOLUTELY NO ONE CAN DIE TO SEE GOOD GOD – LIFE. THEY MUST LIVE A GOOD*

131

LIFE TO SEE GOOD LIFE WHO IS GOOD GOD – GOD.

Life – Good Life should not be at the feet of man.

Life – Good Life should be cherished. But instead of cherishing Good Life, we trample it down – kill it and cry to God – Good God for help – a saving grace.

Why should Good God help us?

We willingly and knowingly destroy life so we have to deal with the consequences. We were the ones to listen to others tell us this god is fine and this one is fine so keep your unclean – dirty gods in the end. Let them save you.

GOD – GOOD GOD CANNOT SAVE YOU IF YOU ARE NOT FOR HIM OR WITH HIM – HIS OWN. HE MUST LEAVE YOU ALONE. YOU WILL SEE THIS IN THE HARVEST HENCE DEATH COMES TO TAKE HIS OWN.

Michelle Jean

I'm back family and for good reason because The Book of Life – Judgement is bothering me. It means there will be another book in the series but I have to address the homosexuality issue in that book. God – Good God I said I was not going to change the book but my spirit compels me to do so. I will not take what I said out of the book because I said IF. ***So because of my vision – her please do not make homosexuals be like the IT THINGS of society.*** I take that back because I know you truly love homosexuals. It's August 11, 2013 Good God and I have to recant my words. But Good God there should be no homosexual agenda because I know you truly love homosexuals. You know what God – Good God let me come out and say it plain and truthfully. *THE DEVIL AND HIS SOCIETY DOES NOT LOVE OR LIKE HOMOSEXUALS BECAUSE YOU TRULY LOVE THEM. YOU GOOD GOD AND GOD IS FEMALE IN THE PHYSICAL REALM THAT IS WHY SOME MEN BEAT WOMEN AND DEGRADE THEM. HOMOSEXUALITY IS A PART OF TRUE NATURE BECAUSE IT IS IN OUR GENES AND THIS IS WHY MAN OR SOME MEMBERS OF HUMANITY TRY TO MANIPULATE THE GENES. THE GENES IS CREATION – GOOD LIFE HENCE MAN OR SOME MEMBERS OF HUMANITY TRY TO DISTORT AND DESTROY THE GENES. Heterosexuals have an agenda and that is to kill and destroy all that is good for SELF, you Good God and humanity.*

133

Because goodness does not conform to their evil ways they destroy, slander and kill goodness – all that is good. A prime example is the manipulation and destruction of our good genes, the food we eat, the water we drink hence the willful destruction of humans and earth itself.

This the homosexual community do not know. Also, they do not know they are blessed and highly favour because some of them do not go to *WHORES HOUSES CALLED CHURCHES, MOSQUES, SYNAGOGUES, SHRINES AND TEMPLES and disrespect you Good God.* They do not buy death and more importantly *THEY DO NOT TRAMPLE YOU DOWN. THEY DO NOT DISRESPECT YOU IN THIS WAY LIKE THE HETEROSEXUALS DO.* Yes those who claim to know you but worship death and praise death instead.

God – Good God, evil – sin do not want homosexuals but you Good God and God need them. They do not desecrate your holy places. The way I look at it Good God is, you are protecting them. When sin does not allow them in their dirty churches or place of worship every homosexual should jump for joy and truly thank you. Homosexuals are more than worthy and this is why you want me to change my words in The Book of Life – Judgement. God – Good God for you I will because cleanliness is you. So

134

please forgive me and I truly repent and recant those words. But Good God and God I said IF but with you it matters not.

Tell me something, how can a dirty preacher or pastor tell anyone who you have in your kingdom – abode?

Can any man or woman see into your abode with their naked eye – eyes that are not clean? So how can any speak on your behalf – tell of your abode?

They know you not but yet they have the audacity to speak for you. When did you say to them speak for me because I am dirty like you?

When did you say to any of them take your book of sin and codes to slander and kill humanity for sin and death?

If a man or woman including child knoweth you not. How can they speak for you and what is in your abode?

The homosexual community need to do them and continue to walk away from the heterosexual community. They the homosexuals have you and it is with you that they must truly stay. They know now that you are truly with them because some do not go in the way of the

135

wicked hence Psalms One is for them. They must continue to stay out of the way of the wicked.

Psalms One says:

1) Blessed is the man that walketh not in the counsel of the ungodly, nor standeth in the way of sinners, nor sitteth in the seat of the scornful.
2) But his delight is in the law of the Lord; and in his law doth he meditate day and night.
3) And he shall be like a tree planted by the rivers of water, that bringeth forth his fruit in his season; his leaf also shall not wither; and whatsoever he doeth shall prosper.
4) The ungodly are not so: but are like the chaff which the wind driveth away.
5) Therefore the ungodly shall not stand in the judgment, nor sinners in the congregation of the righteous.
6) For the Lord knoweth the way of the righteous: but the way of the ungodly shall perish.

The ungodly shall not stand in the congregation of the righteous because they are filthy – dirty. So as a homosexual stay away for these wicked and deceitful people. Do you in a good and true way. Do not act like the heterosexuals because many of us are like onto whores and prostitutes, liars and thieves because men and women made us so. Look at the way we as heterosexuals are behaving and please for the true love of God do not emulate us because many of us will not see God.

We disrespect God by turning homes we say is dedicated onto him into whore houses and gambling houses – casinos. ***We have no respect of God – Good God because we wear our dirty and filthy stinky shoes in houses we say is dedicated to God – Good God. SO TRULY BE THANKFUL THAT THESE WHORE HOUSES REJECT YOU. YOU AS A COMMUNITY (NOT ALL) CAN STAND BEFORE GOD – GOOD GOD AND SAY GOOD GOD AND GOD WE DID NOT DISRESPECT YOU BECAUSE WE DID NOT BUY DEATH NOR DID WE TRAMPLE YOU DOWN IN CHURCHES – WHORE HOUSES WITH OUR DIRTY SHOES.*** *The heterosexual so called church community cannot say this but many of you in the gay and lesbian community can.* So tell me who does God – Good God prefer? Them or you? Truly think and live because you can lift your hand in and to glory – Good God right now and say thank you Good God for protecting and saving me – us. The

137

heterosexual church community cannot say this but you can so truly give God thanks and continue to walk away and do good.

Stop fighting with the heterosexual community for justice because there is no justice in their community. There is no truth or true love in their community because men and women act worse than whores and prostitutes in the eyes of man and God.

Stop vying to become whores liars and deceivers like them. It's not worth it. YOU HAVE GOOD GOD ALREADY DO NOT GIVE HIM UP TO BE APART OF THE DEVIL'S OWN.

Remember good and evil must separate and if you are good stay good and clean because you are a part of Good God's true kingdom.

Do not change you like the It Things to become liars – deceitful sinners. They disgrace God – Good God in every way hence any land or lands that give It Things (transgenders) a home must be destroyed. Thus saith/sayeth the Lord thy God meaning it is so. They are true Sodomites hence their land must be destroyed like Sodom and Gomorrah. This is the law and humanity – humans cannot change this law to please them or anyone. You do not change your sexual orientation – genes and birth record – certificate to say that you are male when you were born a female. You do not change your sexual orientation – genes and birth certificate to say you are a female when you were born a male. You are a sinner and a liar hence no transgender it things are found in God's – Good God's abode because they are an abomination of sin. Not one of them can look upon God – Good God or call upon him because they have done worse in the eyes and sight of God – Good God than the Egyptians – Babylonians, Ethiopians and Religion combined. When you can repent of your sins they (transgender it things) cannot. There is no repentance of sin for a transgender it thing. As for you cross dressers that dress in women's clothing, you are under the category of it things because you knowingly and willingly lie to people. You are neither male or female hence God – Good God has a bone to pick with the lots of you. So repent of your dirty and filthy ways. As homosexuals look at the female gene XX because the XX represents you. Like I've said, no dirty clergy can speak for Good God.

Man there is so many things you need to know so please be proud of you.

So Vladimir Putin, repeal your homosexual law because homosexuals are not Sodomites those disgusting and filthy It Things (transgenders) are. They are the true Sodomites hence any land that gives them legal rights must destroyed like Sodom. Thus saith/sayeth the Lord thy God meaning it is so. They cause men and women, including family to be condemned in the eyes and sight of Good God hence ***DEATH TRULY DO NOT WANT THEM. THEY CONTAMINATE DEATH.***

This is the reason why the churches do not want homosexuals in their whore houses – dead houses because homosexuals stick up for It Things. Those disgusting It Things (transgenders). Like I said, the dead and death nor the whore houses of death wants them because of the contamination and condemnation they bring.

These It Things are deceivers – liars because they say they are male when they are female and vise versa. They are causing you to live your life in a lie and like I said lies are sins punishable by death. Trust me any land that houses them must give them a one way ticket of no return off earth. ***AND NO YOU CANNOT KILL THEM.*** Whichever land say yes they have rights and can live in their land, then you can give them a one way ticket to that land so that they can further contaminate it – that land that gives them asylum. And yes this goes for the doctors and nurses that aided these worse than demons of hell. Their family is also contaminated hence their children – family must leave with them. They are no longer clean – holy – good in the eyes and sight of Good God.

Know that homosexuals are not It Things because like I said, Good God is female in the physical realm. The physical is Good God's abode also. Once the earth is cleaned up you will see the unification of the physical and spiritual. Yes this will take time so truly repeal your ban on gays and lesbians.

Like I've said, no clergy can speak on the behalf of Good God because the clergy have and has done worse in the eyes and sight of Good God hence they are in revelations.

They the clergy cause humanity to commit adultery – sin.

Stop. Because I will not allow you to say no.

EVERY CLERGY MAN OR WOMAN THAT RE-MARRIES A MAN OR WOMAN WITHOUT THEM GETTING A DIVORCE FROM GOOD GOD HAVE AND HAS CAUSED THEM TO SIN HENCE THEY WILL SEE HELL. THERE ARE NO ANDS IFS OR BUTS ABOUT THIS. THEY CAUSED THAT PERSON TO SIN

141

VILE IN THE EYES AND SIGHT OF GOOD GOD.

Hence **HUMANS MUST DIVORCE IN THE EYES AND SIGHT OF MAN AND GOOD GOD. Good God must issue us our divorce decree.** So for those that have died if they were good and they have that one sin on their record there is no way in hell that they are going to get to Good God's kingdom – abode. **They will infinitely and indefinitely never ever forever ever never ever get to Good God's abode.** THEY ARE INFINITELY AND INDEFINITELY GOING TO GO TO HELL AND BURN. This I can take to Good God's bank and bank because it is so. Thus saith/sayeth the Lord thy God meaning it is so. Woo Nelly when it comes to this. I so don't want or need to be any of you.

If the clergy is dirty, **well they are** and they marry you, your marriage will never, infinitely never ever be clean. It is dirty – unclean.
If the clergy buries you meaning commit your body into the grave your body is infinitely and indefinitely dirty - unclean. You take on the sin and sins of that dirty person. He or she was never ever, infinitely never ever ordained by Good God to commit your flesh – body unto him. SO TRULY GOOD LUCK IN THE GRAVE BECAUSE YOU ARE INFINITELY DOOMED. Thus saith/sayeth the Lord thy God meaning it is so.

142

And no people Good God is not heartless. You can still go to him in truth and ask him to divorce you from his record if this has happened – you remarried. And yes this go for committed relationships that have broken up. Don't even think it because a committed relationship carry more clout with Good God than a marriage done by a dirty man or woman.

Like I said, Mr. Putin you cannot tell someone he or she cannot be with this or that person. **THE ONLY ONE THAT CAN DO THIS IS GOOD GOD.** *He did it with Eve and she did not listen hence Eve (Evening) died. He's done it to me. The first time I did not understand what he was trying to tell me hence I learnt the hard way. This is why I stress knowing the good colours of Good God. I tell my children if they see any woman (my daughter does not want to listen hence I know she will learn the hard way) in the colour black coming to them or coming down on them in their dreams to run like a thief in the night because she is unclean.* ***She is coming to take their life.*** *They cannot get involved with this person because* ***this person is their death in the physical world. Stay away and never entertain her or him.***

These clergy say they speak for Good God but yet none can tell you, "thou shalt not kill." War is

143

murder – a sin because you are killing another human being.

None can tell you that if you send another human on the battlefield to kill, you are committing a grave sin in the eyes and sight of Good God hence losing your place with him.

*Yes many leaders do not know this so now you know now do better. **Instead of banning HOMOSEXUALS BAN THE CLERGY** because they are leading humanity down the pathway of death – hell.*

What right do any have to say homosexuality is a sin?

Did Good God tell them specifically homosexuality is a sin? And don't even think of bringing the book of sin to me hence it's called the holy bible. None can say this book is holy because it is death's book – the book of the dead as well as the book of sin.

Masturbation is sin. Why doesn't the clergy tell people this? And yes I was specifically told masturbation is a sin. And this is because of our sinful thoughts when performing the act. And yes people if you are true to masturbation you can tell Good God that you are truthful to the act and you cannot give it up. He Good God will overstand. If you do it (masturbate) without a partner you cannot think of anyone – fantasise about anyone. The sin comes in when you fantasise about someone. Yes it's hard but it is attainable.

Do they (the clergy) not take little boys and girls and have their way with them in some churches?

*Do they the clergy and the members of the church not **DEFILE GOOD GOD AND HIS NAME INCLUDING MORALS?***

What makes the clergy moral when they deal in immorality including death?

They sell humanity death and when the person dies that's when they find out that their triangle has been turned down. They must face hell – go to hell and die. So what makes them (the clergy) holy – good?

Is it the sins that they do that makes them holy? Or is it the death that they sell that makes them holy?

Either way they are not holy hence they too must go to hell and burn because they are truly condemned.

145

Billions are slated to die because of their lies and deceit hence Satan is the head of their domain – whores houses that they call churches.

As for you the homosexual community enough already because I am truly getting tired of you. Live your damned life because I am infinitely sick and tired of this person and that person coming out and saying they are Gay. Many are not gay but it seems it's become a custom to ride on the coat tails of gays. Trust me if you continue to piss me off I will petition Good God against you. But then I can't because I infinitely do not want to see her again, so I will thread lightly. No, Good God don't mess around so stop. He did not put any of you in any damned closet. You'll put yourselves in closets. Stop boxing your damned selves in and live your life. Do you and truly thank Good God for truly blessing you. And yes the hypocrisy has to stop. Yes you've been treated unfairly by the heterosexual community and those people have to pay for their sins. They will pay hence there is hell. I know it is no consolation to many of you that have lost friends and family but make it a consolation hence the harvest comes.

Like I've said before homosexuality is in the spiritual realm. I've seen it. I've never seen male to male homosexuality only female to female but it does not mean there are no male homosexuals in the spiritual realm. There are but they are

146

forbidden to me – meaning for me to see. And no one in the heterosexual community better use this explanation to justify your wrongs because none of you know the spiritual realm like I know it. <u>Good God how do I explain it for humanity – all to comprehend – understand and overstand. Good God the explanation I offer I do not want or need the It Things to use it to justify self because I infinitely and indefinitely know for a fact they are a condemnation onto man and land including you Good God.</u> Okay here goes. Remember I told you I saw the 3 daughters of Satan. In your book of sin – Genesis they are male but in fact they are females. They were the three deaths of Eve (Evening). No that's not a good explanation because I am confusing you and I am so confusing me so scrap that explanation. Death comes to us as male and female and it is death that you have to decipher. Death can show you a female dying but in fact it is a male that dies hence death confuses you. So Good God I am going to leave this explanation alone. Humanity just know that there are male homosexuals in the spiritual realm and like I said, not because I did not see them it does not mean that they are not there. I know for a fact that they are there.

Just know that there are 3x's to one y hence 3xy is a part of our genes. Homosexuality is not a condition, it is not sickness, it's not a disease, it is not unholy, nor is it a sin. Hence we have 3 times more female hormones than we do male hormones.

Stop saying no we don't.

Yes we do. Factor in Mother Earth.

Yes Oh.

So Good God, I hope I explained the truth correctly because I do not want to see this lady come to me again. Hence the correction in this book and my repentance of sin, well words in the New Book of Life – Judgement.

Okay. Since I am on my way of correcting things I have to do this.

Mad Cobra's Defend It. Mad Cobra, I am going to Defend It. *I will infinitely not change my views and words when it comes to this song because the entire Jamaican Government are GUTTER BELLY SEWAGE AND SLIME IN MY BOOK.* They are scum bags of the worst kind to the way they treat their people. **THEY ARE A DISGRACE TO THE BLACK RACE BECAUSE OF WHAT THEY DO UNDER THE NAME OF GOOD GOD AND IN THE LAND OF GOD – GOOD GOD.** I will never apologize to any because I do not class them as **_BLACK OR A PART OF THE BLACK RACE. I KNOW FOR A FACT THEY ARE A PART OF THE RACE OF SIN HENCE THEY ARE BLACK DEVILS – THE DEVIL'S OWN. VAMPIRES AS PETER TOSH SO ELOQUENTLY PUT IT._** They give the ghetto children of Jamaica guns and lie. Say they don't do it – didn't do it and they did it. They tell their police force to kill by any means necessary then turn around and lie to people and say it is not so. **_Not one of them truly love their people because if they did the senseless killings, stealing, raping and murdering of little children would cease._** We say Jamaica is blessed but Jamaica is no longer blessed it is becoming cursed because the government and people of the land made it so. **_NOW THE LAND AND PEOPLE ARE UNCLEAN – DIRTY IN THE EYES AND SIGHT OF GOOD GOD._**

Mad Cobra I truly love Defend It, but I am going to defend it. Dance Hall is not bigger than me or anyone and more importantly Dancehall is not bigger than God – Good God because the **_DEVIL MADE DANCEHALL (the now version of dancehall anyway)._** _Satan owns the dancehall community. UNNU BOW worse than bow cat because nuffa unnu go a foreign and a blow pan man saxophone. Unnu_

149

waane lash out on the gay community. Well mi a lash out and a talk di ting now. Bunch of hypocrites. Nuff a unnu a paid rides – roller coasters fi man hence unnu go roune an roune like a bleeping merry-go-round. Some a unnu a mail order prostitutes including mail order brides for some members of the gay community.

Dancehall has become an abomination unto Good God because it glorifies DEATH – THE DEVIL. Hence Satan owns dancehall and the artists of dancehall.

Dancehall glorifies Satan hence SOME A UNNU, SATAN A UNNU DADDY LITERALLY.

I TRULY LOVE DEFEND IT, **_BUT WHEN IT COMES TO DIS DEM ANYWEH AND MORE IMPORTANTLY MADABLE SICK WITH YOU AND BOUNTY KILLER THE MAN YOU DISSED IN DEFEND IT, THEN I MORE THAN DRAW THE LINE._**

Hence these lines.

TODAY, I AM CALLING ON EVERY DECENT HUMAN BEING AND TRULY GOOD GOD LOVING PEOPLE TO PETITION MADABLE SICK TO BE BANNED INFINITELY AND INDEFINITELY FROM EVERY MUSIC CATALOGUE GLOBALLY. NO DECENT AND TRULY GOD LOVING – GOOD GOD LOVING PERSON WOULD DEFEND AND PLAY THIS GARBAGE THAT YOU AND BOUNTY KILLER CALL A SONG.

THIS SONG HAS AND HAVE GONE ABOVE AND BEYOND PROTOCOL. YOU MORE THAN TOOK IT TO THE LIMIT IN THIS SONG. THIS SONG WAS WILFULLY AND PURPOSEFULLY DONE THUS THE WILLFUL DAMAGE TO HUMANITY ESPECIALLY CHILDREN THAT EMULATE YOU AND BOUNTY KILLER. I TRULY HOPE GOOD GOD NEVER FORGIVES THE BOTH OF YOU

151

FOR IT (THIS SONG). MADABLE SICK GOES AGAINST GOOD LIFE, HENCE GOOD GOD MUST STAND AS WELL AS GO AGAINST YOU AND BOUNTY KILLER INCLUDING EVERY DANCEHALL ARTIST IN THE GLOBE. Yes this includes you Lady Saw and I truly like you. As raunchy as you are, I truly like you because you are capable of so much better hence Heels On High with Shaggy.

Before the song is banned ***TRULY LISTEN TO THE LYRICS AND HEAR WHAT THEY SAY. YOUTUBE MUST BAN THIS SONG BECAUSE NO ONE CAN OR MUST GLORIFY MURDER – THE KILLING OF ANOTHER HUMAN BEING.***

MAD COBRA, I DON'T GIVE A BLEEP IF SATAN GAVE YOU YOUR VISA CARD TO KILL. NOT EVEN SATAN HIMSELF WOULD SAY THIS SHIT. AND NO SATAN, I DO NOT SPEAK FOR YOU. AS SICK AND DISGUSTING AS YOU ARE, YOU WOULD NEVER SAY THIS HENCE "EVIL WILL" THAT URGES PEOPLE ON. YOU ARE MATERIALISTIC. HENCE I KNOW YOUR OFFERINGS IN THE SPIRITUAL WORLD. HENCE YOUR MINIONS ON EARTH. YOU ARE DEVIOUS. HENCE YOU ARE THAT SICK PERSON THAT

PREYS ON HUMANITIES WEAKNESS. YOU ARE DOUBT, HENCE THE MIND GAMES YOU PLAY TO GET YOUR WAY. THE FALSE HOPE AND OFFERINGS THAT YOU GIVE TO TRAP HUMANITY ON A WHOLE.

*COBRA YOU AND BOUNTY KILLER HAVE GONE BEYOND WICKEDNESS – SINFUL IN THIS SONG. SO SINCE SATAN GAVE YOU YOUR VISA CARD TO PROMOTE DISGUSTING AND MURDEROUS LYRICS LIKE THIS, **I AM TRULY ASKING GOD – GOOD GOD AND HUMANITY TO BAN THIS SONG. AS WELL AS BAN YOU AND BOUNTY KILLER AND ALL DANCEHALL ARTIST LIKE YOU THAT PROMOTE DEATH – SIN AND HATRED FROM ALL THE LANDS OF EARTH. SO, ON THE BEHALF OF GOOD GOD, I AM ISSUING YOU AND EVERY DANCEHALL ARTIST THEIR DDC – DEATH'S DEATH CERTIFICATE. DANCEHALL MUST INFINITELY DIE ALONGSIDE ALL OF YOU.** GOOD GOD MUST NOW BAN ALL OF YOUR SONGS FROM HIS RECORD BOOKS BECAUSE YOU AND THE DANCEHALL ARTISTS - COMMUNITY ARE ALL LYRICAL MURDERERS AND MURDERERS THAT HAVE NO RESPECT FOR GOOD LIFE. HENCE JAMAICA HAS AND HAVE BECOME UNCLEAN – DIRTY IN THE SIGHT AND EYES OF GOOD GOD. **NONE OF YOU MUST BE GIVEN VISAS TO GO INTO ANOTHER MANS LAND AND PROMOTE FILTH LIKE THIS.** YOU AND BOUNTY KILLER*

153

ARE WRONG – MORE THAN SINFUL WITH LYRICS SUCH AS MADABLE SICK. ***Trust me what you sing and give the devil he keeps.*** *So Cobra since you said* **SATAN GAVE YOU YOUR VISA** *CARD consider yourself a part of the devils clan. There is no way in hell that you will see Good God because the devil – Satan plays for keeps. He does not dick around with what humanity has given to him whether implied or not.* ***You are his hence your name is in Death's Books. You can thank yourself for that.*** *REMEMBER YOU TOLD THE WORLD AND SATAN THAT* ***YOU HAVE A SOUL COLLECTOR AND THE DEVIL GAVE YOU THIS SOUL COLLECTOR****. So truly good luck to you and your family in HELL.*

Mad Cobra and Bounty Killer children are listening to filth like this and neither one of you are setting good true and honest example for the children of this world. NONE OF YOU CAN DEFEND DANCEHALL WITH LYRICS SUCH AS THIS. IT TURNS MY STOMACH TO SEE WHAT THE LOTS OF YOU ARE ADVOCATING. NO COUNTRY IN THEIR RIGHT MIND CAN GIVE YOU OR ANYONE VISA'S THAT GLORIFY AND PROMOTE DEATH. YOU ARE MORE THAN WRONG WITH THIS SONG.

With this song, Madable Sick the ***Jamaican Government has and have all right and rights to jail your asses and ban dancehall music infinitely and indefinitely.*** You cannot write shit like this nor can you glorify killing. No, all of you need to be banned. This is beyond reckless and sick in anyone's book. This is willful and beyond sinful in the eyes of God – Good God, hence there is no forgiveness on your part for this song. I was into this song and I am glad Good God shielded me from the lyrical content. Trust me I truly listened to it (Madable Sick) and have to say, I am more than disappointed in You and Bounty Killer. ***I truly no longer like Bounty Killer because he not only disappointed me but his dead mother. And yes I can say this because his mother was with him. Note was.*** He too has and have disrespected the people of Jamaica – Black People on a whole when it comes to worse than garbage like Madable Sick. *I refuse to listen to his crap anymore. And I refuse to listen to you anymore because of Madable Sick.* Like I said, you went above and beyond protocol with this song hence I am asking humanity not to buy the song and I am asking ITunes and all song catalogues to ban this song – pull it from their portfolio. All radio and television stations including internet providers must ban this song. ***WE ALL HAVE CHILDREN. WE ARE ALL HUMAN BEINGS AND FOR YOU TO SING A***

155

SONG LIKE THIS IS BEYOND DISRESPECTFUL AND DISGRACEFUL.

*People lose their lives each and every day and songs like this more than hurt. **It spits in the faces of people as well as spit in the faces of families who have lost loved ones to violence. The both of you are damned reckless. No wonder Jamaica has become unclean – dirty in the eyes and sight of Good God.***

Tell me something, *what are you truly saying to the mothers and fathers who have lost their child to gun violence – murder?*

What example are either one of you setting for the younger generation?

Who are you – any of you to profess murder?

When these kids take up the gun and start murdering what say you and killer to them? Get a bleeping life and clue.

BADNESS HURT AND IT DOES HURT LIVES – FAMILIES.

We say children are the future, but how can children be our good future when we have artists like you promoting murder – death?

You and Killer (Bounty Killer) are adults but neither one of you are responsible.

You're both irresponsible hence your stage names – names of death because it is death – murder – killings the both of you advocate.

Yes any of you can rib these books and say pick the beam out of your eye before I pick it out of someone else's. Many of these books have swearing in them but I have never advocated violence against anyone nor will I do it because life is important to all. And like I said, we are the ones to give our lives away to sin.

I'm a parent and a member of society and as a parent and member of society I cannot knowingly condone **SINS – SINFUL AND DEADLY SONGS SUCH AS THIS.** As society – good members of society we have to draw the line and I AM DRAWING THE LINE. **NO RADIO STATION OR DISC JOCKEY CAN PLAY THIS SONG AT ANY FUNCTION – PARTY.** Everyone must ban this song and if they don't **BAN THIS SONG I AM TRULY ASKING GOD – GOOD GOD TO BAN THEM AND THEIR CHILDREN – FAMILY FROM HIS GOOD AND TRUE ABODE –**

157

KINGDOM. Good God must ban their names and take their names out of his good book of life. Come on now. Yes I deleted this song from my music portfolio. My brain is saying I shouldn't, but I cannot listen to the negative side of my brain I have to listen to the good side. Respect is due all the time.

Mad Cobra you are wrong. I cannot give you right for this song because it is a sin in the eyes of Me hence Man and Good God. *This song is beyond offensive and I am asking the Gutta Belly dem in the Jamaica Government to ban this song and if they have to ban you Mad Cobra and Bounty Killer and all Dance Hall Artist, then so be it because you are all wrong.* You cannot glorify death because death did not give humanity life. Death takes life. If you and Bounty Killer like death so much why the hell don't you go live with death and get the hell off God's land? Go the bleep to hell with death and burn since you love death so much. Go. Tell death to take you to hell. You love death so much take his damned train and go. You don't need a ticket to get on board the both of you have his mark already. ***Bounty you have the mark of death which is the MARK OF THE BEAST – YOUR TATTOO AND YOU MAD COBRA SAID SATAN GAVE YOU HIS VISA CARD MEANING YOU TOO HAVE THE MARK OF THE BEAST WHICH IS THE MARK OF DEATH. SO GO TO HELL WITH***

DEATH NOW AND LEAVE DECENT PEOPLE THE HELL ALONE. COME ON NOW. BURN YOU DEMONS OF HELL BECAUSE HELL FIRE IS TRULY WAITING FOR THE BOTH OF YOU. Jamaica need to become clean. *THE NAME JAMAICA MEANS GOD – GOOD GOD MADE ME AND I REFUSE TO MAKE THE DEVIL AND HIS CHILDREN DESTROY MY WONDERFUL HOME AND LAND - HOMELAND.*

JAMAICA DOES NOT STAND FOR DANCE HALL ARTISTS DESTROY ME.
JAMAICA DOES NOT STAND FOR DANCEHALL ARTISTS MADE ME.

LIKE I SAID, IT STANDS FOR *GOD – GOOD GOD MADE ME AND IT IS GOOD GOD AND HIS LAND THAT I MUST DEFEND.*

And no Good God will not sin me for what I said to Bounty and Cobra. If they love death so much, then they must go to hell with death come on now. Who the hell wants death's demons in their land? Go to your fathers land and pollute it. Get the hell out of Jamaica. *I INFINITELY AND TRULY NEED JAMAICA TO BECOME CLEAN SO THAT I CAN GO AND ENJOY MY GOOD LIFE WITH GOOD GOD. HENCE I PETITION GOOD GOD FOR THE LAND AND NOT THE PEOPLE. I MICHELLE KNOW JUST HOW WICKED AND EVIL MY PEOPLE ARE HENCE*

159

DEATH HAS THEM. LIKE I'VE TOLD GOOD GOD, THE EARTH – LAND HAS DONE HIM NOTHING WRONG HENCE DEATH MUST LEAVE THE LAND ALONE. HE DEATH, MUST TAKE HIS WICKED AND EVIL PEOPLE BUT HE CANNOT TAKE THE LAND. COME ON NOW.

And no it does not mean that death cannot the land, he can due to the uncleanliness of the land. Right now death can take the land of Jamaica because of uncleanliness the people making the land unclean.

ONWARDS I GO

If you (Mad Cobra and Bounty) want to sing and glorify slackness get the bleep OFF AND OUT OF JAMAICA BECAUSE IT IS OBVIOUS THAT GOD – GOOD GOD DID NOT MAKE YOU OR ANY OF THESE NASTY STINKING GUTTA BELLY SLIMEY STINKING CESSPOOLS OF RECTOBATES THAT GLORIFY THE DEVIL AND ALL FACETS OF SIN AND EVIL.

None of you represent God – Good God or Jamaica the good land he Good God has and have given us.

160

Like I said, **_we the Black Race are a disgrace in the eyes and sight of Good God. Hence I ask him (Good God) yet again, if it does not repent him to make man – humanity especially the Judas's (Judas Race) that call themselves blacks – black people?_**

Yes the black race can be in an uproar because I call them the Judas's. But none can justify self because all I have to do is take you back to the beginning in the book of sin and point to the original Judas – that being Eve (Evening). Like I said, from her come slap back till now we've been selling out Good God and none can say this cannot be. We must stand good and true with Good God.

White people stop laughing because you are included in this. You too are Judas's hence I do not make any distinction between races. So take your beating because **"OUT OF MANY TRULY ONE PEOPLE – RACE."**

When I look at the videos on YouTube of all the slut dogs that pose up themselves, I hold my head down in shame and disgrace and wish they were never a part of the human race –black community and race. _Hence because of them men of all races can look down on us (women) and call us monkeys and coons, whores and slues. We have no respect for or of self. We have_

161

no self pride. We have become worthless in the eyes of Good God and Man hence sin turn us into cunnu munnu.

Tell me something. What are we truly teaching our children?

Is this what society – the black race have and has become?

No wonder we knoweth not our history or culture because if we did we would not disgrace Good God like this. We would live in pride and true beauty. ***WE ARE A WALKING DISGRACE TO OUR ANCESTORS LITERALLY BECAUSE WE SPIT IN THEIR FACES EACH AND EVERY DAY.***

We have no black pride hence we are worse than slaves to the Babylonian system of things. Thus we kiss the ass of the Babylonians each and every day and bow down to their dead gods like bow cats.

We worship them because it is their dirty and stinking gods we believe in and put our trust in.

NO WONDER HELL IS FULL OF BLACK PEOPLE hence the vision shown to me.

Wi wuse dan pancoot hence drangcrow vomit at the sight of some of us literally.

162

No wonder some of our children are the way they are. Gutta belly raising gutta belly. Have some bleeping ambition. Cu pan unnu to. Some a unnu say unnu come from Kings and Queens and unnu a walking disgrace when it comes to our African ancestry and heritage – pride. ***NONE OF YOU, NOT ONE OF YOU ARE TRUE AFRICANS BECAUSE NOT ONE OF YOU CAN WALK IN THE FOOTSTEPS OF OUR TRUE ANCESTORS. ABSOLUTELY NONE. NOT EVEN ME BECAUSE I'VE SINNED.*** *Hence the Babylonians can write books of crap – shit and give it to you and say it's your history and heritage and the lots of you gobble it up and say YES MAN A DI TRUTH.*

How can watered down crap – shit be the truth of your ancestry?

Africa we say is our home and not even them know their damned history – heritage. How shameful and disgusting – disgraceful.

This is Africa and none know their roots – true history. None can tell you about the truth of Good God – Life. So how the hell can any say they are African's – of Good God? You're all frauds because the true Africans never gave up their roots hence they are living with

163

Good God right now. Many of you are the children of Eve (Evening) hence the Genesis of your book of sin is your true beginning. Come on now. Sin hath a beginning and an end hence sin is your Alpha and Omega – Male and Female.

If you as Africans were so true, none would be following the lies and liars of religion because Good God did not give us religions of men to dirty ourselves and land with or by. Come on now. Get a bleeping clue and let go the Babylonian System of things and live if you can.

WE ARE AFRICANS BUT YET WE DO NOT KNOW OUR TRUE HISTORY. HOW RIDICULOUS. No wonder other races can laugh at us and call us fools.

KNOW YOUR DAMNED HISTORY AND CULTURE IF YOU CAN.

No wonder old people say write some a unnu name pan bulla cake an unnu grap it dung without knowing unnu name write pan it.

We say we love our heritage. Whoops I forgot there is no truth in love hence none of you can

TRULY LOVE YOUR BLACK HERITAGE – GOD AND GOOD GOD. And you the White Race this goes for you too because I told you about Black and that some of you fall under the banner of Black as in the Jamaica Flag literally, so take your punishment too. You are not excluded and I refuse to exclude some of you. Some of you *are BLACKER THAN BLACK with your good deeds and goodness.* So take your punishment because *you are BLACK WHETHER YOU LIKE IT OR NOT.* Blackness is not about skin colour it's about good honest and true deeds – truth. So kiss it when some of you say you are not black because you are. *EVERYONE LOOKING AT SKIN COLOUR LIKE SKIN COLOUR CAN GET YOU INTO GOOD GOD'S ABODE.*

GET REAL PEOPLE. THERE ARE NO SECTIONS IN GOOD GOD'S ABODE FOR THIS NATIONALITY OR THAT NATIONALITY. And don't even come to me with the mountain. Good God had to show me the mountain this way so that I can refer it back to you.

THERE ARE NO SECTIONS IN GOOD GOD'S ABODE FOR THIS SKIN COLOUR OR THAT SKIN COLOUR.

THERE ARE NO SECTIONS IN GOOD GOD'S ABODE FOR THIS RELIGION OR THAT RELIGION.

165

THERE ARE NOT SECTIONS IN GOOD GOD'S ABODE FOR THIS HATED AND THAT HATRED. COME ON NOW.

Like I said, ***we are responsible for our sins. We are the ones that must answer for them because there are no lawyers in Hell or in Good God's Abode.*** Our sins are recorded in our record book and at the time of death our record is taken out. Hence our record is handed to us in the grave. This is why I tell you over and over again ***THE LIFE YOU LIVE IN THE LIVING DETERMINES WHERE YOU GO IN DEATH – THE GRAVE.***

IF YOU CANNOT FORGIVE A MAN IN THE LIVING, YOU CANNOT FORGIVE HIM OR HER IN DEATH.

Hence if you have more sins on your slate in the living – physical there is no way in hell you are going to go see Good God. The god you will see is Death and greater Death – the death of death. So to all that say they are going to die and see Good God. I say unto you yet again, "truly good luck with that" because I know for an infinite fact you

166

will never ever see Good God. You will see death and die in hell with death.

And Vladimir Putin know this; a man or woman that have been separated from his wife or husband and sleeps with another woman or man commits adultery. You are charged with sin because you did commit willful sin – wrong.

THOU SHALT NOT COMMIT ADULTERY.

A man or woman that is separated cannot engage in a relationship with another person. He or she must obtain a divorce decree from Good God and Man before he or she can engage in another relationship. This is the law of Good God hence you are not in accordance with the law and laws of him (Good God). You too are guilty like the next man. So how can you or anyone charge the next man or woman for sin when you too have sinned also?

YOU CAST THE FIRST STONE NOW I AM THROWING THE STONE BACK AT YOU IN THE NAME AND TRUTH OF GOOD GOD.

*Your clergy that you so believe in, also committed sin because they failed you and Good God. **They failed to advise you of your sin.** And no it matters not if you are talking to the person. You are to respect your union. **And no it matters not***

167

if your wife said it was okay to have someone else. *If she told you to have someone else – it is okay, she too have and has committed a vile sin and yes, viler than you. She cannot give you permission to take another because she is more than violating your union. She is sinning worse that you because she is permitting you to commit a sin on top of a sin.* <u>Hence her sins are doubled in the eyes and sight of Good God and she must be punished worse than you.</u> *Thus saith/ sayeth the Lord thy God meaning it is so. It is law and no human being can change this because it is written.* <u>So wrong cannot charge a person for wrong if that person have not committed anything wrong. You and your clergy are the wrong ones hence you must repeal Russia's Homosexual Law.</u> *Remember Russia has been warned hence this book of death. You can save Russia, so do that which is right and good in the eyes and sight of Good God because as it is you are listening to death (your clergy). Religion hath nothing to do with Good God. All you have to do is read Revelations and what it said about the seven churches. So if Good God is truly against them,* <u>*WHAT MAKES THEM HOLY AND OF GOOD GOD?*</u>

ONWARDS I GO

No one can petition for you in the grave if that person is not ordained by Good God to do so and

I've told you this. And in order for this to happen, the person must be living. Hence Good God sends you his messengers in the living to warn you as well as tell you which pathway to follow in goodness and in truth. He or she cannot be dead nor can he or she live as the dead. And gifts are different if you are going to go there because I know some of you will go there. *When I say gifts, I'm talking about the language and message of Good God.* Good God cannot change your record book to please you or anyone. If your triangle points down then it must stay down. You belong to death and no one can change this. *The upright triangle is sacred because it is the ORDER OF GOOD GOD and Life – Good Life.* Hence you cannot interlock the upright triangle with the downward triangle. **IT IS INFINITELY AND INDEFINITELY FORBIDDEN.** To do this (interlock the upright and downward triangle) means you are married to death and Life cannot marry death. **WHEN LIFE MARRIES DEATH IT MEANS YOU DIE – YOU ARE GOING TO DIE.** *Death is your husband and or wife hence Good God cannot save you. Good God cannot break this bond because this is the bond you chose. You choose and chose death over life.*

I'VE TOLD YOU IT IS BETTER TO KNOW THE TRUTH IN THE LIVING RATHER THAN WAIT

169

UNTIL YOU ARE IN THE GRAVE BECAUSE YOU WILL HEAR "TOO LATE."

WHAT YOU CAN CHANGE IN THE LIVING YOU CANNOT CHANGE IN DEATH. YOU NEED TO KNOW THIS.

Like I said, we are the ones to disrespect God – Good God and when things do not work out for us with sin we come crying back to him (Good God).

So Mad Cobra, I Defend It because you infinitely did wrong. Children and Young kids do listen and class musicians like you as heroes. Children do scream out when they see some of you because in a way they can relate to you. Some children want to become like some of you and it's a shame that some of you screw up our children badly. ***Children and people do listen and it's up to you to teach and educate right.*** Your fans you are accountable for in my book hence I am holding you accountable for them. ***No artist can say their fans made them then turn around and give them dirty***

food – the meat of pork – swine to eat. When you do this your fans become defiled hence Good God becomes defiled also. Truly listen to Madable Sick and tell me personally if this song was justified. Certain books I've written and Good God refuse to let me publish them because the actions in them are not right. When the time is right then I will be able to publish these books. Meaning I have to edit them of the wrongs in them. Yes people these are my early books – the days when I was just starting out hence they are unpublished. Also Mad Cobra, I am not a saint. I am just like the next man that has flaws meaning make mistakes. People truly care especially children hence they flock to some of your concerts. Man if I could get screaming fans like some of you, I'd be more than happy because I would be more than blessed and highly favoured in more ways than one. So please do right and change with the death thing. It is not warranted. This is the time for the harvest. Hence dancehall is not bigger than this harvest that is coming. Many of you are going to cry like a bitch when shortage of food and water hits. Many of you are going to cry like a bitch when financial strains more than hit unnu. *HENCE NO MONEY A GO RUN FI SOME A UNNU.* And yes it would be well deserved because now you will know just how deceiving the devil can be. More importantly how deceiving the devil is. Hence Satan is the biggest *GIVER BACKER*

171

TAKER THERE IS WHEN IT COMES TO FINANCES – MONEY AND MATERIAL GAIN. Some a unnu a go wish di island sink when wusarra food and wata shortage hit unnu. Drangcrow nyam unnu suppa soon. Just watch and see. Like I said, ***Jamaica has become unclean in the sight of Good God and mi naah sarry fi none a unnu.*** Unnu di people and government mash up Jamaica. Unnu sign unnu lives literally over to death. Hence death soon comes and woe be unto the lots of you. Like I said, when you sing songs like Madable Sick, as a human being that truly loves God – Good God I have to draw the line. You are not setting a good example for you or your children. Honestly, I am furious with you because this song (Madable Sick) was truly uncalled for. You have children and what if someone was to use a ---- and ---- them? How would you like it? *What's good for the goose is not good for the gander.* This is why I lash out at Jamaicans and the Black Society because I am angry at some of crap you artist tell our people to do. Right now the government (s) of the land (earth) has and have a right to ban dancehall and charge the lots of you for murder and treason against humanity – the people of the earth – world.

Many of you dancehall artists in Jamaica are to blame for the escalating bloodshed on the land. ***Many of you blame the government and yes***

172

the government of Jamaica is to blame because men – gang members can rape thirteen year olds and walk the land freely. This is the society and reality of Jamaica right now.

Hence the land and people are unclean in the eyes and sight of God – Good God literally.

TELL MI SOMETHING, UNNU HA SHAME?

TELL MI SOMETHING, UNNU NO SHAME?

UNNU HA AMBITION?
UNNU HA PRIDE?
UNNU HA DIGNITY?

Good God literally said unnu unclean. Hence I can safely say

173

unnu no worthy. Unnu done hence JamaicaF. Jamaica and the people of Jamaica have and has failed Good God literally. Hence there is no Jamaican pride.

Unnu fi wol unnu head down in shame and disgrace because another black land and people bites the dust. Have and has gone down to hell literally.

And to add this footnote, none a unnu can blame the WHITE MAN FOR THIS. <u>*YOU CAN ALL INFINITELY AND INDEFINITELY BLAME SELF.*</u>

ONWARDS I GO

Children have no worth hence many are raped and slaughtered like animals and discarded at the road side.

The government care not for the people hence ***JAMAICA HAS BECOME THE MODERN DAY SODOM AND GOMARRAH OF OUR TIME. The land and people must burn hence death awaits its toll.*** Only a few more senseless killings then death will walk and sink the land hence Sodom and Gomorrah – Jamaica will be no more. Yes it's sad but the dancehall community must be blamed as well. *Some of you advocate bleaching of the skin and people follow unnu and do it without knowing that they are hell bound. Anyone that bleaches the skin to look like sin literally has no home and place with Good God.* ***THEIR TRIANGLE IS TURNED DOWN AND NOTHING THAT THEY DO IN THE LIVING CAN OR WILL CHANGE THIS – SAVE THEM IN THE END. THEY HAVE THEIR DDC HENCE HELL IS THERE HOME.***

These people can thank some of you gutta belly dancehall artists for this. *You lead them – your fans to hell hence they have no escape – return when death takes them.* **Hence as fans you must truly know what you are doing and who you are following. Some of these artists** *lead you straight to hell. You cannot give up your souls – good life so freely to death because there is no escaping hell.* Like I've said, **no one has ever escaped from hell.** *Absolutely no one can, because we are the ones to give our lives to death. Once you give your life to death you cannot retrieve it in the grave – hell.* **NO ONE CAN NOT EVEN GOOD GOD HIMSELF.** *So truly learn now before it's too late.* Like I've said, many of us have our <u>DC and this DC can change to a GLC and/or a GGLC – Good Life Certificate and/or a Good God Life Certificate.</u> *This is truly up to you which one you choose as of this day.* Like I said, **<u>there are different stages to the mountain it is how you choose and or chose to get there.</u>**

<u>HELL IS REAL AND NO ONE HAS EVER ESCAPED HELL. NO ONE NOT EVEN SATAN AND DEATH.</u> So truly think about your life because your soul – spirit is yours to keep and life is truly worth living. Like I said, it's wrong for us to give our souls over willingly to people that brings you to hell – your death. **<u>LIFE IS MORE THAN WORTH IT DEATH ISN'T.</u>**

UNNU DONE PREE SATAN INCLUDING YOU HENCE YOU DEFEND DADDY DEMON. **<u>He's sick and that is why he wants to emulate Malcolm X.</u>** He wants to be that variable that changes humanity. ***But he cannot change humanity or his people for the better. He can only change them for the worse hence the skin bleaching he advocates to look like sin literally.*** Malcolm X was not a part of Good God's plan (good portfolio) because he was a part of the devil's clan, ***hence Islam. He was a Muslim hence he was a variable of death – one of the changing faces of death.*** X is unknown many say. But this is a lie. X will always be known to God and his children hence Good God's children know about X. It matters not the mathematics or the deception of the devil's clan we know X hence X is not unknown to us. X is represented by the number 24 in the English Alphabet and language. 24 represents the 4 and 20 elders in your book of sin as well as your 24 hour clock – army time or army watch. Yes the time for war people. 24 also represent the time frame of sin to deceive humanity on earth. 24 also represent Satan and his 3 daughters hence 6+6+6+6 = 24 which is 3xy. All Malcolm X was telling Good God's children was that he was an agent of death – Satan. ***Hence BLACK DEATH.*** So daddy demon is a clown that wants to pick up where Malcolm X left off but it cannot work. He daddy demon is not Muslim and I guess this is why he has his demon book that some are flocking to buy. ***And please people do not associate the 3xy to homosexuals because if you do I will more***

177

than school you with the genes and the mountain of Good God so truly don't go there. I AM INFINTELY AND TRULY WARNING YOU.

Satan and his people use the 3xy for evil but I've shown you the good in it.

Satan and his people mock good hence you have his demons mocking Good God and the eye in the upright triangle. So as evil mocks Good God, he mocks his children also. Homosexuals do not bring forth evil children, heterosexuals do because many do not want children. And they are the ones Good God look at. They are not polluting the earth with evil. Period.

Dancehall cannot run from its murderous and evil ways - tendencies.

Cobra, like I told the Jamaican government, I will destroy them before I let them destroy Good God and his land. You are no exception to this. I more than infinitely truly love Good God and before you destroy him I will destroy you and the dancehall community. *I refuse to let demons like you destroy and sink Jamaica. If the people of Jamaica want you and the dancehall community to continue to destroy them, then that's fine. But I will not have you continue to* defile the land of Good God. Jamaica is Good God's land not the devil's land – home hence Ja – Mai – Ca. **_You did not create Jamaica, Good God did and I will not allow you or anyone to destroy his place – creation which is my place of birth._** Take your slackness someplace else. This goes for some of dem dancehall females wey can't DJ also. People unnu tone def? No for real, unnu tone def? I guess unnu wi buy crap just to feel like unnu a paate a di crowd. Buy good and sensible music that compliments you and stop wasting your money on garbage. Crap that not even the dead and drangcrow want to listen to. Only demons listen to some of these artists. Demons love them and di bag a nise dem so called sin sorry sing. Hence they sing and DJ crap for demons. Come on now. None can stand in the court and courts of Good God hence they praise and worship Satan and bow down to demons.

Evil reel us in in every way and we buy it. Hence sin has so much power over humanity – man and the Jamaican society as a whole.

We buy into sin and when we *GO TO HELL AND BURN WE HALLA AN A CRY FI GOD – GOOD GOD FOR A SAVING GRACE. YOU BUY HELL SO STAY IN HELL AND BURN.* Come on now. Good God will not save you because you disrespected him in every which way in life. So why call upon

179

him when the demon's of hell is feasting on your spirit?

Don't like the fire do you?

Good, now stop calling out to Good God fi help yu.

You believed in death.

Did all for death so live in death.

You were told death is real.

I told you when you snub your toe it's not the flesh that feels the pain it's the spirit. The spirit is trying to warn you – tell you that the pain of hell is infinitely worse than this and you would not listen.

I know hell and I've said not even Satan I would want to go there. But he made his choice so let him burn – continue to burn and feel his pain of hell. ***LIKE I'VE SAID, GOOD GOD LOCKS NO ONE OUT OF HIS ABODE. WE ARE THE ONES TO LOCK OURSELVES OUT.*** Good God does not hate the Babylonians because they too can receive life. All they have to do is repent of their sins and live in truth. ***TRUTH IS EVERLASTING LIFE*** and ***I will not petition for none.*** (A Babylonian). *I refuse to no matter how kind and* good they are. I am not accountable for them. I am only accountable for the seeds – the good people and children of Good God. No, I refuse to hate any Babylonian hence they are an abomination unto me by choice – my good will and good choice. ***They are liars and deceivers hence what they did to Eve (Evening) and Moses.*** Go back to the book of sin and read what they did to the children of Israel when Moses went up to the mount (mountain). *What did Moses come back and see?* So because of this, *they are infinitely not on the Mountain of Good God* because they caused Good God's people to sin vile. Hence many died right there and then. Death took them (the people) because they became a part of death's own. Much like us today hence the harvest comes. We are not different ***HENCE GOOD GOD INFINITELY CANNOT TRUST HUMANITY. WE'VE FAILED HIM TIME AND TIME AGAIN.*** When he helps us, many of us go to the houses of sin and say, "thank you Jesus for helping me", "thank you Jesus for saving me." ***You all give death thanks and glory for what Good God has and have done hence you mock Good God and spit in his face.*** So because of this, *NO CHRISTIAN, NO JEW, NO GENTILE, NO MUSLIM, NO BUDDIST, NO JEHOVAH'S WITNESS, INFINITELY AND INDEFINITELY NO CATHOLIC, NO CHURCH OF GOD, NO ZIONIST, NO RASTA, NO NATURIST, NO ATHEISTS, NO SINNER*

INCLUDING VOODOO PRIESTS AND PRIESTESS, OBEAHMAN AND WOMAN, WITCH AND WARLOCK – YOU NAME IT CANNOT AND WILL NOT SEE GOOD GOD. THEY MUST AND WILL SEE DEATH. NONE CAN OR WILL ENTER THE ABODE OF GOOD GOD. HELL IS YOUR HOME AND IT IS HELL THAT YOU MUST BURN IN BEFORE YOUR EVENTUAL DEATH.

The harvest that is coming hath nothing to do with Good God. *It hath to do with man – humanity and your sins.* We are the ones to cause this because we commit willful sins every day. We refuse to give up sin hence death comes to collect his pay. And trust me infinitely on this, **_death must and will collect his pay. Death and Sin did not sin brutally in the eyes and sight of Good God man – humanity did._**

*SO WHEN SOME OF YOU ARE GOING TO SAY, "GOD, SATAN MADE ME DO IT." GOOD LUCK WITH THAT BECAUSE **SATAN CANNOT MAKE YOU DO SOMETHING YOU DON'T WANT TO DO.** HE SATAN GAVE YOU AN OFFERING AND YOU ACCEPTED HIS OFFERINGS, SO BLAME YOU NOT HIM. COME ON NOW. And to say "God, Satan made me do it", you are committing sin. You are lying to Good God hence you will go down to hell to see sin and death because "you knowingly lied to Good God in front of his face." Don't even say it because you have. You may not*

182

see Good God but he see's you hence your record – slate of truth – good and evil.

We as humans buy sin hence the Churches of sin that sell death. I have no clue why anyone would think that when they sin they are going to live up to see Good God? ***YOU ARE GOING TO GO DOWN AND SEE HELL – DEATH. YOU ARE GOING TO BECOME A SLAVE TO DEATH HENCE ABDULLAH.*** You must pay for death and that is why you go to church. Hence you pay death with your money and your lives.

No one can be a servant or witness of God – Good God hence Good God I am coming to you again. I am tired of this woman – Jehovah's Witness coming to my door. I keep telling her I am not interested in her pamphlets and she keeps coming and I am getting pissed off at her and you. Again she came to give me her pamphlets and I told her I am okay which is fine. But when she lied and said I must be new in my apartment that pissed me off because I've not changed my short and incredibly grey grey hair. My boobies still hang down and I still wear the same glasses. So to you the Jehovah's Witnesses that keep disturbing people, stop because no one is disturbing you. No one can be witnesses to Good God, ***you can only be witnesses to death.*** Hence you believe in Christ

– a man that did not exist. Enough is enough with you.

LEARN THIS BECAUSE I AM PISSED. NO RELIGION ON THE FACE OF THIS PLANET CAN SAVE MAN – HUMANITY BECAUSE GOD – GOOD GOD IS WITH NONE OF YOU. READ REVELATIONS OF YOUR BIBLE. IT TELLS YOU THERE ARE 7 CHURCHES AND GOD – GOOD GOD HAS A BONE TO PICK WITH ALL OF YOU. YOU'RE ALL LIARS AND DECEIVERS THAT LIE ON GOOD GOD AS WELL AS TRAMPLE HIM DOWN WITH YOUR DIRTY AND FILTHY SHOES. YOU DO NOT RESPECT GOOD GOD HENCE GOOD GOD HATH NO RESPECT FOR ANY OF YOU.

I do not need the dirty and stinking gods of BABYLON you do. I infinitely have good and true life already so keep the hell away from my door. Keep your stinking creebay creebay frounzy, armshouse, dead god and gods. I am more than fine with mine. I don't want nor do I need yours because your god cannot save me. I am the one to save me – self. My sweet, more than sweet Good God is saving me. I am a true and living testament of that.

184

IF RELIGION COULD SAVE HUMANITY, HUMANITY WOULDN'T BE SINNING AND BUYING DEATH. THEY WOULD LIVE FOR LIFE IN A GOOD TRUE AND CLEAN WAY.

IF RELIGION COULD SAVE MAN – HUMANITY, THERE WOULD BE NO SIN IN THIS WORLD.

IF RELIGION COULD SAVE MAN – HUMANITY, NONE OF YOU WOULD BE TEACHING AND PREACHING DAILY FROM THE BOOK OF SIN. YES, THE FORBIDDEN BOOK OF GOOD GOD HENCE THE FORBIDDEN TREE.

GOOD GOD NEVER GAVE US THE BOOK OF SIN MAN DID HENCE MAN – HUMANITY SIN AGAINST GOOD GOD RECKLESS DAILY.

IF RELIGION COULD SAVE MAN – HUMANITY, HUMANITY WOULD KNOW TO TRULY PASS OVER DEATH AND LIVE.

GOODNESS AND TRUTH, CLEANLINESS AND HONESTY IS WHAT GOOD GOD REQUIRES OF EACH HUMAN BEING AND WE CANNOT DO THAT BECAUSE RELIGION SELL LIES HENCE

185

WE BUY SIN AND DIE. DULY NOTE THE 10% THAT RELIGIOUS LEADERS TELL HUMANITY THEY HAVE TO PAY. YOU'RE THIEVES OF THE WORST KIND HENCE NONE OF YOU ARE FOUND IN GOOD GOD'S BOOK OF LIFE.

KEEP YOUR DAMNED CONDEMNATION OF DEATH AND LEAVE ME AND GOOD GOD THE HELL ALONE BECAUSE IT IS HE THAT I TRULY, MORE THAN TRULY AND INFINITELY NEED AND INFINITELY TRULY LOVE. So don't come around with your sly way and expect me to disrespect Good God because I would never turn from him for anyone. I know the truth and it is the truth that I am trying to live by. *FAMILY I AM NOT FULLY THERE YET BUT ONE DAY I WILL GET THERE. AND TRUST ME NOTHING CAN OR WILL HOLD ME DOWN OR BACK BECAUSE I WILL BE TRULY CLEAN GOOD AND PERFECT IN THE EYES OF GOOD GOD. ALL MY SINS WOULD BE PAID FOR IN FULL. This is what I strive for hence I cling to Good God – God.*

All of you can give up Good God hence the time of Noah. So, if I am the only one left on the face of this planet. I will more than truly thank Good God and say Abay to the rest of humanity amongst other things. In so doing, if I am the only one left on the planet, I ask God – Good God not to replenish the earth. Let earth clean itself up and once earth is clean good and true only good spirits – good people in energy form including him Good God must live on the earth forever ever if it's his desire. Wickedness including wicked and evil people must be gone from earth. Come on now. Like I said, I am like each and every one of you. I have flaws but I do my best not to disrespect Good God. I am rough in language – words but that's my spirit sometimes. I cuss but that is my nature. Anyone that knows me can tell you from mi likkle bit mi a cuss. I will defend the truth with my words hence I defend God – Good God and his land. Like I've said over and over again, if you don't want Good God leave him the hell alone. Get the bleep off earth because Satan did not create it. Good God created earth hence humanity knows not about atoms and the power and strength of them. What humanity sees is just a tat because there are atoms that telescopes cannot see hence the power of Good God.

Truss mi you noa wha mek mi omit this part and figet it because I infinitely know the end of the black demons – the black race is at hand hence hell is full of black people and recruiting more.

We cannot teach our children to hate and kill and not expect them to go out and hate and kill. Come on now.

We teach our children wrongs and say it's right. When our children do the wrong things we tell them to do, we reprimand them and say they did wrong. You taught wrong in the first place so the onus is on you the person that taught and teach wrong.

IT'S THE SAME WITH GOVERNMENT. You tell us – society it is wrong to kill and you charge us. Send us to jail for killing including stealing but yet you do the same and you do not go to jail. You are not charged for murder and stealing. You send young boys and girls on the battlefield to murder someone from another land and to you this is fine. You also tell them to rob the next man's land of his wealth and when your citizens do the same in your land you charge them for theft and murder. You teach wrong and we see you doing wrong but yet no one can judge you or charge you for wrong. Do we not see you doing wrong and follow your wrongs? So how the hell can you charge your citizens for wrongs? If you do not set good examples for your citizens to follow how the hell can we follow them (good examples)? ***Well let me tell you this. BECAUSE OF YOUR WILLFUL ACTS OF SIN YOUR LAND HAS AND HAVE BEEN JUDGED HENCE THE HARVEST COMES.***

WOE BE UNTO MAN AND LAND IN THIS HARVEST. I feel sorry for none because like I

188

said, we are the ones to give sin power. Now that sin has and have destroyed us by signing our lives over to death, we are going to cry to Good God like David and Jesus and say, "***my god, my god why hath thou forsaken me,***" and like I said, **GOD – GOOD GOD DID NOT FORSAKE MAN, MAN – HUMANITY ARE THE ONES TO FORSAKE GOOD GOD.** This is our reality and we have to live with it. We are the ones to condemn ourselves to a lifetime of spiritual slavery in hell before our eventual death. We as humans know right from wrong. But instead of walking away from our wrongs we continue to do them and expect someone to save us. Good God cannot save us from willful sins because they were purposely done.

Let me ask you this, for all of you that go to the Obeah man and woman to get fame and fortune.

HOW COME DI OBEAH MAN AND WOMAN INCLUDING VOODOO PRIEST AND PRIESTESS AND LODGE MAN CAN'T OBEAH DEATH SO THAT DEATH DOES NOT COME?

All a unnu claim sey unnu ha power but none can obeah death?

None can turn back death.

189

None can obeah the next guzzu man or science man or lodge man from harming another man or woman's child with their slackness.

All you can do is cast so called spells by using your book of sin to turn down and destroy.

All of you say you have power but yet none can stop the destruction of humanity – man – this harvest that's coming.

None can repair the ozone that is being depleted by our sins.

None can save a sick child by destroying the cancer indefinitely.

None can destroy all forms of cancer forever ever so that it does not take the flesh of man – the life of the flesh.

None can save humanity from the death of death.

Like I said, we claim but we are the ones to give evil power.

If we don't go to the obeah man and woman can they have power? Take your money and plunge your spirit further into hell.

If we do not buy the books and records of sinful and wicked people, can they have power?

If we do not buy into sin and do the will of sin, can sin have power over you and me?

If we do not marry sin, can sin have control and power over us – our day to day lives?

If we do not walk in the way of sin, can sin kill us – hand us over to death?

If you answer no to the questions above, then you are on your way. So on this day slowly move away from sin. As to the homosexual community, sin does not like you so stop trying to integrate into sin's society. Like I said, God – Good God has been protecting you so stay protected and do good by you. Have your own good true and honest schools, doctors, dentists, hospital, movie houses, department stores, theatres and keep the sex to a minimal in your movies because I am disgusted and sick of seeing scantily clothe people on television and on the internet. There are kids in society hence teach them the good values and morals of Good God. Infinitely and indefinitely do not teach children including the adults of your community the dirty and stinking immorality of the heterosexual community. The heterosexual community do not represent Good God you do because GOOD GOD IS ***FEMALE IN THE PHYSICAL WORLD.*** This is the best way I can

191

explain it. ***GOD – GOOD GOD DOES NOT DISCRIMATE AGAINST SEXUALITY. WHAT GOOD GOD DISLIKE IS FOR US AS HUMANS TO HAVE THIS AND THAT SEXUAL PARTNER OR DIFFERENT SEXUAL PARTNERS IN OUR RELATIONSHIP AT THE SAME TIME.*** *Meaning if you are with one person stay with that one person.*

*And infinitely yes, yes, yes **Polygamy is an infinite sin.** Good God never told anyone polygamy was clean – lawful. It is unlawful. Infinitely and indefinitely forbidden. So wooooooo Nelly, infinitely truly good luck to some on you and this one (polygamy). Nasty men – perverts, sex addicts are the ones to legalize polygamy. It is nasty hence the many nasty bacteria of men and women. This is why many of us stink below lacka ten day tunda. Trust me Good God is going to deal with your whoring and nasty asses soon.*

Laade mi hot. Good God polygamy for real. You more than infinitely truly love everything – all things good and clean and these nasty Things are saying polygamy is clean. No wonder the whoring and abominable ways of the Babylonians cannot stop. BUT IT'S INFINITELY DONE NOW. HENCE THE HARVEST.

Michelle Jean

192

Oh before I go. This morning August 21, 2013, I had some awkward dreams. Before I get into the dreams I have to say congratulations to Jay-Z, his wife, Kanye West, P. Diddy and all that are associated with these people including, Oprah, Tyler Perry, their staff and companies just to name a few.

People, I did tell you the harvest is almost here but this dream is so weird. I saw this land, I cannot tell you the name of the country nor can I tell you about the man because I was not focused on the dream. All I can tell you is that this man planted crops and when he went to harvest it, (pulled up his crop) he got nothing but dirt. The bunch he pulled up out of the ground was dirt. The ground or land did not yield to him anything. All the earth or ground yielded him was dirt. And yes the land – earth was dry. Weird because I've never seen the earth yielded dirt before. Oh well I just have to wait and see which land – country this happens to.

Man there is so many things I saw but can't fully relate them because I do not fully remember them. I know I saw water yet again but I cannot tell you how high up in the earth the water was this time. All I know is Canada got rain to wet the land hence Canada is wet – has water and even this dream is weird because I did not see rain coming down. All I saw was the sidewalk and grass wet.

As for the congratulations above people. Wow. Jay-Z you and your wife was the main focus of the dream especially you. This is a spiritual dream as well people. Hence in this dream this man was trying to kill me but it did not work. I escaped hence I ended up in this place where Jay-Z and his wife, Kanye West and P. Diddy was. In the dream Jay-Z's wife was smiling. Much like the smile she had on her face in the picture she and Jay-Z took with their daughter in the true North - Canada. And I will reserve the daughter part because I still say that's not a real child – baby. There's something wrong somewhere with this child hence drones for which some of us call clones. That's just my opinion. Dat dey jacket more than cut to fit to backside. Dat dey jacket dey more than a match. It ovafit. That's all I got to say. A true clone dat. Dat dey fish dey caane get wey. Ee hook tight – right. Wow.

On to the dream

I dreamt that Jay-Z received the **_MARK OF THE BEAST_** on his hand. **_He literally had the mark._** The mark is a tattoo that is on his right hand (if you are facing him). Oh man let me get this right. I don't know men's clothing or shirts.

194

The shirt was a T-shirt and the mark was up on his arm but the t-shirt did not fully cover the mark because I saw some of it. I cannot tell you the exact marking but he did get the mark of the beast and his wife was happy. ***And yes he was in full black.*** Because I saw the mark, I was telling him in the dream that he was a part of Satan's kingdom – clan. I was explaining to him about it and suffice it to say he did not like me telling him what he was. Trust me a gun came into play. You know those guns that they play Russian Roulette with. The ones you have to put the bullet in and spin. That type of gun. No the person that had the gun did not pull the trigger nor did it go off. Like I said I was telling him about the mark of the beast and he did not believe me so in the end he said he was going to check it out.

So Jay-Z, Jay-Z's wife, Kanye West, P. Diddy and all who associate with you are now a part of the Satanic Society of Sin and Death literally. In the dream Satan gave you Jay-Z power hence I say congratulations. Woe be unto man because you have been marked. You have your DDC the mark of death. You have death's mark hence your friends and associates have it too. ***SATAN GAVE YOU POWER TO FURTHER DECIEVE AND KILL HENCE THIS ASPECT OF REVELATIONS IS COMPETE. HENCE WOE BE UNTO MAN WHEN THIS DEVIL IS DONE.***

Good luck, truly good luck in hell because you are infinitely and indefinitely truly there now. **<u>YES IN HELL.</u>**

<u>*This was what you and your wife were vying for. Now it is confirmed and you now have confirmation of this.*</u> Satan gave you the power you wanted. You have been marked hence you are infinitely a part of the devil's own. There is no escaping this judgement for you or anyone. So truly good luck. People this is what I saw and this is what I am relating back to you.

Know this, no one is bigger than Good God not even Satan himself. Because in the end, what Satan gives to you via his seed – children, he does take it back in the end. In the dream Kanye West and P. Diddy did not receive the mark but because they were there and apart of the ritual...no not ritual. They were there with you Jay Z. So because they were there with you they too are a part of Satan's Club – Kingdom. They are just like you – Satan's own. Hence your children and girlfriends are a part of the CLUB OF DEATH. They have their DDC's. Like I said, I did not see Kanye West, P. Diddy and your wife with the mark of the beast. You were the one to get it (the mark of the beast) but it does not mean they do not have theirs. They could have gotten theirs prior to you. So if you got the mark they got theirs too because they were there with you.

So good luck because the devil is going to have a field day with all of you. You and your family have and has been indoctrinated in hell hence hell is now your home along with your friends and family. Woe Nelly you going to burn. Wow. Don't want to be in any of your shoes because ***SATAN WON OVER THE LOTS OF YOU BLACK DEVILS.*** Know this. There is no saving grace for any of you because ***you all HAVE THE MARK OF THE BEAST AND THERE IS NOTHING ANY OF YOU CAN DO ABOUT IT.*** You've been stamped on your right hand so good luck with that.

And no, you cannot sue me because this is what I saw hence I am relaying the dream back to you as I saw it. I will not change the dream to suit you or anyone because to do so would be a lie on my part. And no matter the death threats and coming after me and my family, I will infinitely not alter the dream the suit you or anyone.

Good God showed me this hence I am telling you this. You know what you are doing hence you are high up in your organization. A part from Satan and his children, you are the first human that I saw with the mark of the beast. I've seen many things but you are the first confirmed case. Meaning you actually got the mark of Satan – the mark of the beast. You got what you wanted so truly good luck like I said.

So good luck with that because you will never see Good God or his abode. Neither will your wife, P. Diddy, Kanye West and your associates.

Like I said, we as black people are the ones to give up Good God to accept the devil's own.

Oh just a footnote......never mind because I know Good God is truly on my side.

Michelle Jean

Family I so want to close off this book but can't. I so do not know why I am lingering. Oh well I guess this is just me procrastinating.

But truth be known I have to get this off my chest because something is just not right in California.

America is it me or is there a suicide epidemic in Hollywood?

What the hell is in the water and food for so many people to be committing suicide?

Do these people not know suicide is evil's way of killing people? Meaning suicide is evil will – the demonic way of killing you. Suicide is death all around and there is no repentance or forgiveness for this act. Once you take your life you are gone meaning you are hell bound. Suicide is death's true calling for some because it is engrained in our evil will and trust me this will of death is strong, more potent than the will of sex to a large degree.

I guess I now comprehend the "so as a man thinketh so shall he do" message I got. But yet I still disagree with this statement because human Will is strong and it can be extremely deadly. So Hollywood, I ask you now, what's up with the suicides all of a sudden? Good life is

199

worth living hence clean up your acts and start living clean. Wow. Come on now.

America do something because your land is becoming death's playing field and if you do not nip it in the bud the casualties in your country will fireball – skyrocket. Hence you will not have a need to go to war because your war will be against **_DEATH HIMSELF LITERALLY._**

Some of you stop living above your means and start living within your means and pay down your personal debts please. Do it slowly so that death cannot hold you accountable.

It's amazing how I read about how some of you black artists are being evicted. You'll made money but none prepared for the future. The entertainment industry is not loyal to anyone anymore because Satan bought out the global entertainment contracts worldwide. *Satan owns some of these billionaires and trust me he must get paid somehow. Hence all he gives you is for naught.* **_Goodness does not deteriorate sin does. Hence sin does everything in its power to keep going._** *The heads of these corporations do not care about quality anymore. They care about their bottom line. Making more money hence quality of music and film has and have become a thing of the past. All they give is a quick fix then it's over. Hence we are living in a hurry* *come up and quick fix society that caters to wants and not needs. Now tell me do you need a house here there and everywhere?*

Do you need 500 or even a thousand pair of shoes? Wow. Tell me when do you find time to wear these shoes? Oh I forgot the lucrative social life and shoes to match the outfit. So scrap this one.

Ten to thirty cars if not more. I can't understand or comprehend. Four or five yes but not thirty. Oh speaking of cars Vladimir Putin I know you hate my guts for what I said above. That's okay because I do not hate you I truly love you hence your whip – ride – car is mine. I am laying claim to it. I truly love the front of your ride but not the back. No people have you seen the front of this man's whip – car. I'm a weird person people but I am gushing about the front of this man's limo hence I claim his car in the name of Good God. I want and need to go to Russia and test drive this car. <u>Vladimir I issue Russia a challenge. If I become rich I want my good and more than fine godly and luxury whip – car and ride to come from Russia.</u> Keep the frontal design of your limo but redesign the back. Family, I am so blown away by Vladimir Putin's limo. It's different original and huge – big. Hence I know now why Russians like everything tall and big. Sorry people but I am so getting carried away. And

201

Russia *I NEED MY CAR TO BE TRULY SOLAR THAT EMITS NO HARMFUL GASES OR CHEMICALS INTO THE ENVIRONMENT. Got to keep my life and ride – car clean and true to Good God. Come on now. The color black will do because I so can't picture another color for this car.*

Onwards I go because I am so getting carried away with Russian cars. Move over Russian men there's a new king in town – the King Car well in my case the Queen of Queens – Queen Car. The new BWW – Black Woman's Wheels.

It's authentic.
Original

Russian made.
It's bold
It's beautiful

It's me
The car made for Michelle Jean
It's stately
Refined
Powerful
Yes over fifteen hundred horses

Now that's a state car for me and only me.

Michelle Jean

People, I am crazy and can go overboard with things that catches my eyes. Things that say yeah that's me. I found my calling in this case I found my luxury car.

This limo is the luxury car of all luxury cars. All other cars pale in comparison to this car. People I truly love the front of this car. I truly love cars especially big cars but this car takes more than the cake for me. Nothing can outshine this car because I've found my true whip – car – stately car.

I better stop, I better stop. I only saw the picture of this car people, hence I so need to see the front of this limo in person. I am so overly excited about this car and I so hope I am not disappointed in person when I see it if I get to see it. I know pictures lie hence I need to see this car in person. I need to be truly excited in person not just from a picture stand point. And Mr. Putin, if I do get a chance to behold this true beauty (your limo) it had better be shiny and pretty as the picture or I will be mad at you. You would have disappointed me. Russia would have disappointed me. Yes I truly hate disappointments.

Wow people onwards I go again because I've just lost some of you with my excited rant but I so can't help it.

203

If you as a billionaire think you are immune or going to be immune to this harvest you had better think again.

Like I said above, I dreamt the man yielding dirt. So if this man is yielding dirt, the earth has and have stopped producing – giving or yielding food to humanity.

When this happens pharmaceutical companies will be affected hence they will not find herbs to make medicine (s) for the sick. I am going to draw the correlation to this dream and my other dream. You know what, I won't do it – make the correlation because I would be wrong. 1.3 billion people died of incurable cancer hence I cannot correlate this dream to that dream.

Onwards I go

Grocery shelves will become empty because there will be no food from the ground.

And because the ground yielded no food there is no water. The land was dry hence no rainfall.

So because there will be no food or water humanity will die of hunger and thirst – starvation. ***This is our reality no matter how rich we are.*** Like I said, I saw the lava ¼ way the earth and woe be unto man – humanity when it gets full way. Nothing we do can or will save us. *This is why I tell you if you are living good and clean for Good God including self and family you have nothing to worry about.* Good God will infinitely never forsake his people despite the struggles.

When we think he's not there he's there.

When all hope is gone he gives us hope – truth – good life.

Know that the harvest is not for Good God's people. ***This harvest is for the devil's people.***

Evil required a time to deceive and bring humanity to their knees and that time frame was 24000 years. ***Evil failed because Good God only needed one and he found her. Don't look at me people because the one to save humanity must live clean. She must live clean. If she does not live clean she cannot save humanity. I was not told it was me.*** Like I said, *I more than truly love Good God and I will defend him at all costs with my words but I would never lift a finger to hurt anyone purposely or maliciously.*

I refuse to fight toe to toe like a boxer with anyone nor will I tell anyone to lift up arms against the next person. I refuse to do it. If you as a person violate my space and I keep warning you not to and you constantly bug me and cause me harm, then after numerous warning, I am going to go to the police and ask them to intervene. If that does not work, I am going to cut a nice piece of guava stick and I am going to beat you up like a bitch with it. As Jamaicans would say Mi a go gi yu one F--- lick with it. The police cannot charge me for assault because you continued to interfere with me after you've had several warnings. Trust me, I have no use for a gun or a fist. My guava stick is just fine. And if I can't find a nice piece of guava stick then the Jamaican Buss Mi will do because yu a go ben up wen mi done. So truly leave me the bleep alone. What I see is what I see hence I relate them back to you. It is up to you to accept the true word of Good God or reject them. LIKE I SAID, ***THE DEVIL HAD HIS TALK AND GOOD GOD IS TALKING NOW.*** He Good God is our ark and covenant so take heed because this harvest is going to be brutal for humanity. He Good God will advise you his children which good lands to be in so if ***MAMA AFRICA CONTINUE TO DICK AROUND WITH THEIR LAND AND FUTURE THEN SO BE IT.*** If Africa is not suitable then maybe – just maybe Russia will be. If Russia isn't suitable then maybe Iceland will be. Trust me you will know so that you can flee to the land and lands Good God need you to be in. And yes this is why remnants of black civilization is in every land on earth. Yes we created the universe but we are also the ones to destroy it due to trusting the wrong people. We the black race are a trusting set of people and this cannot change because in a nut shell what humanity values is not what we value. ***And no people, I am not talking about the fake ass black race I am talking about Good God's true people – children.***

And if you say White this or that, slap yourself and call yourself stupid because some of you fall under the banner of Black. *I do not like to differentiate when I speak of colour when it comes to God's – Good God's people because Good God does not differentiate between us.* And don't go there with the mountain either because I gave you the explanation earlier. If you as whites want to segregate yourself then go right ahead but truth is, **you can't** hence the Ying and Yang.

Skin colour has nothing to do with Good God it hath to do with death; the distinction between physical and spiritual death hence the Ying and Yang. Life and death on another and life and true life on the next.

Now I've gone too far.

207

Oh Robin Thicke, T.I and Pharrell drop the lawsuit you've filed against Marvin Gaye's family. This lawsuit is childish and unwarranted. Either I am tone def (deaf) or I've lost my knack for music. There is no similarity to the Marvin Gaye song Got To Give It Up and Blurred Lines except for the cow bells. And that's standard in music given the program and instrument you use. This is my perspective. If you were to look at K.C and the Sunshine Band you can draw the correlation. Your argument is implied meaning you guys wanted to emulate Marvin Gaye's Got To Give It Up. You cannot sue a person for an implied thought or action. You have to copy the lyrics and beat word for word and this is not the case so stop with the stupidity.

If you did cheat this man (Marvin Gaye) then wow you guys are good thieves because I cannot pick up on any similarity with the two songs apart from the cow bells. So truly get over yourselves and move on. The controversy is not worth it. Give credit where credit is due because as writers and artists even fashion designers we do take from each other – mimic each other sometimes. ***GOOD ART FEEDS OFF GOOD ART AND TAKE IT TO THE NEXT LEVEL.*** *A perfect example of this is Shaggy's song It Wasn't Me and Tyrone Davis's song It Sure Wasn't Me.*

Different songs same message. Shaggy's song just have a different twist.

Some of our works are original and some are borrowed – emulated like I've shown you in this book. This is why I push certain songs because they have true meaning and they are good. As long as Shaggy and Lady Saw, Beres Hammond and Fred Hammond, Toots and the Maytels, Damian Marley, Prince, Tyrese, Romain Virgo, Mr. Vegas+ sing good music and come out with good music I will endorse them (the song not person).

*(Lady Saw this is for you. I should have done this above but because of laziness I am not going to go back above. I so need to end this book and for some strange reason I cannot. Any way. Like I said, I like you but you have to truly look into yourself and your music. I truly love your smile and this is why I like you. Like I said, you can do so much better and you are capable of so much better. <u>By you going to sing gospel you are telling Good God that you are a part of death.</u> It's not that Good God does not want you to have a child – children, you are the one to hinder yourself with your wrongs – songs. **<u>You cannot sell prostitution in your songs and think Good God is going to be pleased with you.</u>** Women are not prostitutes. Yes I've called women slut dogs and whores because they act like one and*

are one hence their actions. <u>You condone prostitution and sell prostitution hence you do not respect your vagina – the womb of life.</u> So because you have no respect for the womb – life, Good God cannot permit you to bring forth a child. Now you know the truth so do better. Clean your act and songs up. Like I said by you going to sing gospel will not make you clean. <u>You are making yourself unclean further.</u> Once you clean up yourself as well as your life for the better Good God will open up your womb and bless you with a good child if you ask him for one. You must ask him for a good and clean child, an obedient child that will always be truthful and true to him. You must keep that child clean as well as teach him or her about goodness and cleanliness. This you must ask for in goodness and in truth and you have to keep your good word to Good God.

I use pictures from the internet and like I said and will forever say, once I make it, I will be more than happy to compensate those people for using their art. I do not own them and I've used them without permission. It does not make me right but because I do not know how to find these people I use their artwork in hopes that people will see their art and purchase them. No, I did not explain myself correctly. At any rate like I said, I will compensate these people for using their artwork but the compensation must be within reason. Someone cannot say they need billions when the artwork is only worth hundreds or a couple thousands. Hence I know the lawyers that will nudge and that is why I leave them in the good hands of Good God. People, greed will come into play with some but I fret not about them. *A man's work is a man's work hence we are to truly give credit where credit is due.* Like I said, *I do not own any artwork. I use them to make a point and let people know there are good works out there. I will endorse good and clean works. Hence I don't say I am going to use you. I have to be led there – to that place before I can use that picture.*

Good music is also a key to good and true life because there are meanings – messages behind good music as well as in the music. Good God uses musicians to deliver his message hence we have messengers such as ***Bob Marley and Peter Tosh***. Their music will live on forever because they were a part of Good God's portfolio of messengers. They did their job hence I am doing mine.

I've delivered my message and when my time comes I must go like them.

We do not all get music some get books. Some get ways to educate you like ***Marcus Mosiah Garvey*** did, and he too was a part of Good God's portfolio of messengers.

None failed God because they did that which was required of them.

Humanity – man failed Good God because humanity did not listen. You want death hence death.

The rich man will die like the poor man hence Solomon lost it all, David lost it all; your so-called Jesus who never had it lost it all because of Christianity and Religion and so forth. Christians are going to die people because they believe in death all around. They drink wine and say it's the blood of death Christos – Jesus. They eat flesh and say it's the flesh of Christos – Jesus.

All that is going to happen to humanity – death's children has nothing to do with Good God. It has all to do with sin because it is our sins that take us to hell and kill us.

No one can run from death hence good life lives forevermore. **_TRUTH IS THE KEY TO LIFE AND IF YOU DON'T LIVE GOOD AND TRUE, THERE WILL BE NO SAVING GRACE FOR YOU OR ANYONE._**

Good God never told us to sin.

212

Good God never said go this way and that way to find me – get to me.

Good God never told us to take up the nasty ways of the Babylonians to drive us away from him.

Good God never said participate in animal or human sacrifices to drive him away from us and us away from him.

Good God never said have two three four or even six or seven wives and commit adultery to drive us from him and him from us.

Good God told us adultery is a sin. Hence we are to abide by this law.

When we say we are with him Good God and then go into churches of sin to defile ourselves and worship their gods we are committing adultery.

If you are true to Good God and truly know him no one can rock you because you are true to him.

If you are true to Good God no one can take you from him no matter how hard they try.

Like I said, Good God was with me in the storms I faced in life and I refuse to be ungrateful to him. I know who I have in earth and in the spiritual realm hence I cannot give up on Good God.

<u>I know about head blows because evil spirits use head blows to kill you in the living.</u>

Some people have indents in their heads at death and morticians cannot explain it. Baby dead inna dem sleep an dem sey a crib death. Pity they don't know the forces of evil hence ***MEN IN BLACK OR DEATH IN BLACK***. (Infinitely and indefinitely **<u>NO CORRELATION</u>** to the movie).

I've seen death hence I know death and female death. ***<u>Female black death</u>*** is who the messengers of God do not want to piss off. Female death, we cannot piss off hence my homeland don't know what a clock a go strike dem. And on this note mi done – gone.

Michelle Jean.

21